Translation and Multilingual Natural Language Processing

Editors: Oliver Czulo (Universität Leipzig), Silvia Hansen-Schirra (Johannes Gutenberg-Universität Mainz), Reinhard Rapp (Johannes Gutenberg-Universität Mainz)

In this series:

1. Fantinuoli, Claudio & Federico Zanettin (eds.). New directions in corpus-based translation studies.

2. Hansen-Schirra, Silvia & Sambor Grucza (eds.). Eyetracking and Applied Linguistics.

3. Neumann, Stella, Oliver Čulo & Silvia Hansen-Schirra (eds.). Annotation, exploitation and evaluation of parallel corpora: TC3 I.

4. Czulo, Oliver & Silvia Hansen-Schirra (eds.). Crossroads between Contrastive Linguistics, Translation Studies and Machine Translation: TC3 II.

5. Rehm, Georg, Felix Sasaki, Daniel Stein & Andreas Witt (eds.). Language technologies for a multilingual Europe: TC3 III.

6. Menzel, Katrin, Ekaterina Lapshinova-Koltunski & Kerstin Anna Kunz (eds.). New perspectives on cohesion and coherence: Implications for translation.

7. Hansen-Schirra, Silvia, Oliver Czulo & Sascha Hofmann (eds). Empirical modelling of translation and interpreting.

8. Svoboda, Tomáš, Łucja Biel & Krzysztof Łoboda (eds.). Quality aspects in institutional translation.

9. Fox, Wendy. Can integrated titles improve the viewing experience? Investigating the impact of subtitling on the reception and enjoyment of film using eye tracking and questionnaire data.

10. Moran, Steven & Michael Cysouw. The Unicode cookbook for linguists: Managing writing systems using orthography profiles.

11. Fantinuoli, Claudio (ed.). Interpreting and technology.

ISSN: 2364-8899

Interpreting and technology

Edited by
Claudio Fantinuoli

Fantinuoli, Claudio (ed.). 2018. *Interpreting and technology* (Translation and Multilingual Natural Language Processing 11). Berlin: Language Science Press.

This title can be downloaded at:
http://langsci-press.org/catalog/book/209
© 2018, the authors
Published under the Creative Commons Attribution 4.0 Licence (CC BY 4.0):
http://creativecommons.org/licenses/by/4.0/
ISBN: 978-3-96110-161-0 (Digital)
       978-3-96110-162-7 (Hardcover)

ISSN: 2364-8899
DOI:10.5281/zenodo.1493281
Source code available from www.github.com/langsci/209
Collaborative reading: paperhive.org/documents/remote?type=langsci&id=209

Cover and concept of design: Ulrike Harbort
Typesetting: Felix Kopecky
Illustration: Sebastian Nordhoff
Proofreading: Amir Ghorbanpour, Andreas Hölzl, Bojana Đorđević, Caroline Rossi, Daniil Bondarenko, Elen Le Foll, Gerald Delahunty, Ivica Jeđud, Jeroen van de Weijer, Katja Politt, Jean Nitzke, Paulson Skerrit, Sarah Signer, Trinka D'Cunha & Viola Wiegand
Fonts: Linux Libertine, Libertinus Math, Arimo, DejaVu Sans Mono
Typesetting software: XƎLATEX

Language Science Press
Unter den Linden 6
10099 Berlin, Germany
langsci-press.org

Storage and cataloguing done by FU Berlin

Contents

1 Interpreting and technology: The upcoming technological turn
Claudio Fantinuoli   1

2 Simultaneous interpretation of numbers and the impact of technological support
Bart Desmet, Mieke Vandierendonck & Bart Defrancq   13

3 An exploratory study on CAI tools in simultaneous interpreting: Theoretical framework and stimulus validation
Bianca Prandi   29

4 Experimenting with computer-assisted interpreter training tools for the development of self-assessment skills: National Parliament of RSA
Elizabeth Deysel & Harold Lesch   61

5 Technologies and role-space: How videoconference interpreting affects the court interpreter's perception of her role
Jerome Devaux   91

6 Present? Remote? Remotely present! New technological approaches to remote simultaneous conference interpreting
Klaus Ziegler & Sebastiano Gigliobianco   119

Index   141

Chapter 1

Interpreting and technology: The upcoming technological turn

Claudio Fantinuoli
University of Mainz

1 Introduction

The topic of technology is not new in the context of interpreting. However, recent advances in interpreting-related technologies are attracting increasing interest from both scholars and practitioners. This volume aims at exploring key issues, approaches and challenges in the interplay of interpreting and technology, a domain of investigation that is still underrepresented in the field of Interpreting Studies. The contributions to this volume focus on topics in the area of computer-assisted and remote interpreting, both in the conference as well as in the court setting, and report on experimental studies.

To the best of my knowledge, this is the first book entirely dedicated to this subject. Its publication should not be considered a point of arrival in research work on interpretation and technology, but rather as an occasion to give new momentum to the analysis of a topic that is both current and complex. In this field further in-depth research is necessary in order to better understand the past and future impact of technology on interpretation, on the one hand, and to prepare future generations of interpreters to adapt to a constantly changing market, on the other.

2 Setting technology into the interpreting perspective

When compared to written translation or other language professions, the advances in information and communication technology have had a modest impact

Claudio Fantinuoli. 2018. Interpreting and technology: The upcoming technological turn. In Claudio Fantinuoli (ed.), *Interpreting and technology*, 1–12. Berlin: Language Science Press. DOI:10.5281/zenodo.1493289

on interpreting so far. In its long history, however, interpreting has not been immune to technological innovations. On the contrary, it has gone through at least two major technological breakthroughs with disruptive effects on the profession in both cases.

The first breakthrough was the introduction of wired systems for speech transmission that led to the rise of simultaneous interpreting (SI). First attempts in this direction were reported in the early 1920s, with a patent filed by IBM and its adoption at the Sixth Congress of the Comintern in the former Soviet Union and at the International Labour Conference. This technology acquired broader visibility during the post war Nuremberg trials and was adopted since then in all international organizations. Although the cognitive process of translating while listening to the source speech was not new (chuchotage has been probably around forever), the invention of simultaneous interpretation equipment radically changed the way interpretation was delivered on a daily basis. This technological breakthrough also had an impact on social status and self-perception of interpreters. At the beginning, interpreters feared a loss of quality in their performance and perceived the relegation into interpreting booths and the need to abandon the stage they used to share with diplomats as a worsening of the prestige associated to the profession and, consequently, of their social status. In reality, the broad adoption of SI together with the increasing demand for interpreting services due to geopolitical changes in the second half of the 20th century led to a professionalization of the whole sector and, in turn, to a general improvement of the occupational status of interpreters.[1]

The second technological breakthrough that has affected interpreting practice is the Internet. The emerging of the Web in the 1990s radically changed interpreters' relation to knowledge and its acquisition. Since preparation is one of the fundamental aspects of interpreting (Gile 2009), as it is crucial to fill the linguistic and knowledge gap between event participants and interpreters, the impact of this technology on the profession has been extraordinary. The Web is the most comprehensive and accessible repository of textual material available in many languages and on many topics. Interpreters use it in a lot of different ways, for example to conduct exploratory research before they receive actual conference material (Chang et al. 2018), to create specialized corpora for linguistic analyses (Fantinuoli 2017a; 2018b; Xu 2018) or simply to find translations for specialized terms.

---

[1] For a brief history of interpreting, see for example Takeda & Baigorri Jalón (2016) while for an overview of the social-status of simultaneous interpreters, see Gentile (2013).

1 Interpreting and technology: The upcoming technological turn

Search engines, in particular, have become the privileged door to knowledge (Finn 2017). They are used to discern right from wrong, good from bad, or, in the limited scope of interpreting, to fill knowledge gaps, confirm translation hypotheses, find definitions, and so forth. Thanks to the undeniable advantages of having this wealth of information available with a simple click of the mouse, the Web has become by right the most familiar working environment for translators and interpreters (Zanettin 2002). The Web (and digital devices) has changed not only our habits, but has influenced also our cognitive behaviour, for example through the modification of our reading patterns. Different form printed documents, which are commonly read line by line, digital documents are mostly scanned through in search for key terms or to get a general overview (Pernice 2017). Since there is evidence that this change influences aspects of learning such as recall, comprehension and retention of knowledge (Ross et al. 2017), it is reasonable to assume that the digitization of information has had consequences on interpreting and its underlying subprocesses, especially in the pre-event phase of preparation. The magnitude of this change, however, is still not completely understood as no empirical investigation has been carried out so far to assess this in interpreting.

Currently, interpreting might be on the verge of a third breakthrough which I will call, for lack of a better term, the technological turn in interpreting. Bigger by one order of magnitude if compared to the first two breakthroughs, its pervasiveness and the changes that it may bring about could reach a level that has the potential to radically change the profession.[2] Not only could this lead to a transformation of the interpreting ecosystem in all its complexity, but it is reasonable to assume that it may have a significant impact on many socio- economic aspects related to the profession, from the way it is perceived by the general public to the status and working conditions of interpreters. In order to explore the reasons for and the potential consequences of this technological turn, it is first necessary to briefly introduce the interpreting-related technologies that lie at the core of this discussion.

---

[2]Referring to Hegel, Galimberti affirms that "When a phenomenon grows *quantitatively*, there is not only an increase in quantity, but there is also a radical change in *quality*. Hegel provides a very simple example: if I pull out one hair, I am one who has hair, if I pull out two hairs I am one who has hair, if I pull out all of my hair I am bald. There is, therefore, a qualitative change for the simple quantitative increase of a gesture" (2009: 215) (translation by the author).

3 Interpreting-related technologies

There are three main areas that will play a central role in this technological turn: computer-assisted (CAI), remote (RI), and machine interpreting (MI).

Computer-assisted interpreting can be defined as a form of oral translation in which a human interpreter makes use of computer software designed to support and facilitate some aspects of the interpreting task with the goal to increase quality and – to a minor extend – productivity (Fantinuoli 2018a). Among others, CAI tools are designed to assist interpreters in the creation of glossaries by means of integrating a wide range of terminology resources, in looking up terms or entities in an ergonomic way, and in extracting useful information from preparatory documents, to name but a few. They can make use of advanced Natural Language Process features, such as automatic terminology extraction, key topics identification, summarization, automatic speech recognition, and so forth.[3]

The most evident reason behind the creation of CAI tools is the ambition to improve the interpreters' work experience, by relieving them of the burden of some of the most time-consuming tasks (such as the creation and organization of terminology) and by supporting them in carrying out numerous activities, from the retrieval of preparatory documents to their analysis in a way appropriate to their profession. By improving the working experience of interpreters, both during preparation and during the very act of interpreting, CAI tools ultimately aim at increasing the quality of the interpreting performance. Being an integral part of the interpreting process (suffice it to think of the most extreme case of accessing terminological information during simultaneous interpretation), they are directly linked to and may have an influence on the cognitive processes underlying the central tasks of interpreting.

Remote interpreting is a broad concept which is commonly used to refer to forms of interpreter-mediated communication delivered by means of information and communication technology. It is not a monolithic notion, but it can rather be used to designate different settings and modalities, for example when all event participants are gathered at one place while the interpreters are located at a different venue, or when the interpreter and one of the interlocutors are both present at the same place. As far as technology is concerned, RI can be carried out by means of different solutions, from simple telephone to advanced videoconference equipment.

Up until now RI has been used mainly to provide remote consecutive interpreting services, for example in the healthcare or judicial sector, while in other

---

[3]For some examples of advanced use of Natural Language Processing applications in CAI tools, see Fantinuoli (2017b) and Stewart et al. (2018).

contexts, such as conference interpreting, RI has been scarcely deployed.[4] The limited adoption of RI has to do both with limitations of the technologies available and with the complex cognitive and communicative processes underlying interpreting. Tests conducted on remote simultaneous interpreting (RSI), for instance, have highlighted, among others, issues in the quality of the audio/video signals, the partial loss of contextual information due to remoteness, and psychological factors, such as fatigue, higher levels of stress and loss of motivation and concentration. In the area of dialogue interpreting, issues like turn taking, alienation and stress have been found to be particularly significant.[5]

Technological progress is, however, removing technical barriers to remote interpreting which is becoming a viable solution for many stakeholders in need to cut costs and increase service availability. The increasing demand for liaison and consecutive interpreting services, for example for refugees, has already led to the adoption of this technology by many public institutions.[6] This may apply soon also to the context of simultaneous interpreting. Since empirical tests have shown that it is possible to perform, under certain circumstances, remote simultaneous interpretation without breaching professional associations' codes, ISO standards or other related norms applicable to interpretation (Causo 2011: 202), the number of enterprises offering platforms for RI both in the form of interpreting hubs, i.e. professional environments with booths, high-quality consoles, technicians, etc., and in the form of solutions for home offices has dramatically increased. The scale of its adoption, however, is still unknown.

Machine interpreting (MI), also known as automatic speech translation, automatic interpreting or speech-to-speech translation, is the technology that allows the translation of spoken texts from one language to another by means of a computer program. MI is a technology that aims at replacing human interpreters and is in this respect very different to the other two interpreting-related technologies, since they are designed to assist human interpreters in their work (CAI) or to change the way they deliver their service (RI). It combines at least three technologies to perform the task: automatic speech recognition (ASR), to transcribe the oral speech into written text, machine translation (MT), and speech-to-text synthesis (STT), to generate an audible version in the target language.

Although MI is still very far from achieving the ambitious promise of a comparable quality output as human interpreters, considerable improvements have

---

[4] One notable exception is the use of RI in television interpretation.
[5] For a bibliographical overview, see Andres & Falk (2009).
[6] For an example of adoption in 2016 by the German Federal Office for Migration and Refugees, see http://www.bamf.de/DE/DasBAMF/BAMFdigital/Video-Dolmetscher/video-dolmetscher-node.html

been made over the last few years. This is due to the latest developments in several machine learning technologies: ASR based on neural networks, for example, is quicker and more precise than ever while deep neural machine translation has reached unprecedented quality in terms of precision and fluency of the target language output. First prototypes of MI have been presented after long years of research in the field of natural language processing, such as the real-time automatic speech translation system for university lectures implemented at the Karlsruhe Institute of Technology (Müller et al. 2016), or have been brought on the market by technology giants, such as Google (Pixel Buds) or Microsoft (Skype Translator).

The success of these systems has been quite modest so far as they fail to achieve the goal of quality and usability even for the most basic real scenarios in which interpreting is needed. The creation of machine interpreting systems is so challenging for several reasons, both at a technical and at a communicative level. On the technical side, quality of automatic translation and issues in the latency and flexibility of speech recognition as well as noise tolerance and speaker independence, to name but a few, exponentially increase the sources of errors and inaccuracies. On the communicative side, MI systems suffer from not being able to work – as yet - with cotext and context or to translate all the information that is not explicitly coded verbally, such as the speaker's attitude, world references, etc. However, the advances in machine learning are producing encouraging results not only in machine translation (resolving issues of lexical, syntactic, semantic and anaphoric ambiguity, to name but a few), but also in many related fields, such as sentiment analysis, attitude identification, and so forth. In the near future, the integration of these applications into MI may increase its quality, making it more "intelligent" and increasing its quality to a point where its use, at least in some contexts, could start to be conceivable.

4 The upcoming technological turn

There is some evidence that the profession is heading towards a technological turn. First of all, the interpreting-related solutions brought about by new advances in information and communication technologies as well as in natural language processing are growing in number, and the speed of change is significantly faster than it was in the past. In the three areas indicated above, companies are investing time and effort in order to launch an ever increasing number of software and devices on the market, thus reacting to users' demands but also creating new ones.

1 Interpreting and technology: The upcoming technological turn

More important, however, is the fact that interpreting is caught up in fundamental and pervasive changes of the labor market due to technological developments, in particular to digitization and automation, which are creating new patterns of work organization (Huws 2016; Neufeind et al. 2018). Interpreting is not immune to these developments. Notwithstanding the relatively small economic impact of the interpreting sector,[7] the pressure to embrace new technologies may soon increase. Not only the market, but also society, which, as Besnier (2012) points out is literally obsessed with technology, may have enough persuasive power to impose a paradigm change on the profession, no matter the personal attitudes towards it and the concerns about potential consequences on quality, working conditions and so forth. If the technological adoption is quite unproblematic in the area of CAI tools, as their use will influence only (micro)processes of the interpreting activity, but will not have any relevant socio-economic impact, for example on the labor market, the situation may become more complex as far as RI and MI are concerned.

The real impact of these two technologies on the medium and long run is difficult to predict. In the case of RI, for example, there is no doubt that it will offer increased opportunities for work in new market segments, leading to a productivity effect, i.e. an increase in the demand for labor that arises due to technological progress. However, chances are that it may also lead to a deterioration of working conditions. The large-scale adoption of new interpreting-related technologies, such as RI, could drive a process of commoditization of interpretation, intensifying the effects of modern paradigms of labor organization, such as outsourcing (which is already typical in the language sector and many other professions of the tertiary sector). For example, it is plausible to think that RI, at least in some market segments, may bring about a partial depersonification of the service provider. When services become more impersonal and uniform from the buyers' point of view, they tend to buy the cheapest, initiating a downward spiral of economic decline and, ultimately, de-professionalisation of the industry.

In this scenario, machine interpreting may further contribute to accelerate this process. Although MI is still in its infancy and the limits of current implementations are clear, there is no doubt that the fast evolution of this technology will have both a long-term impact in some areas of the profession (if/when the technology reaches a mature status it may put at risks interpreters jobs), and, most interestingly, a short-term impact in the public perception of the activity

---

[7] Suffice it to compare interpreting with the written translation industry to see the importance of economic aspects in technology adoption. The cost-cutting potential of computer-assisted translation (CAT) tools in the 1990s and, more recently, of machine translation in the translator's workspace have forced the large-scale adoption of such tools, irrespective of the personal attitude of translators towards these innovations.

performed by professional interpreters (and consequently in the perception of different stakeholders). This, in turn, may under certain circumstances undermine the status of the profession well before the time MI will actually represent a potential threat to human interpreters.

It is probably for this or similar fears that interpreting technologies have been traditionally welcomed with a general attitude of aversion and skepticism by professionals. This hostility generally takes the form of arguments in defence of quality, in the case of RI, or in defence of the exclusive intellectual dimension of the interpreting activity, in the case of CAI. Its real motivation is, however, the natural feeling of insecurity and fear of technologically induced changes and, consequently, the need to pursue a legitimate and strategic goal, the defence of the interests of the category (Pym 2011).

Paradoxically, a balanced and responsible adoption of interpreting technologies could be fruitful to reverse such negative trends. Looking at the broader picture, the most promising approach is to use technological advances for the benefit of the interpreters, reaping the advantages and opportunities offered by technology while preventing the risk to be dominated by it and by the consequences that arise from its use. There is no doubt that interpreting is about to go through a transformation phase driven by socio-technical change. In this context, the profession urgently needs to play an active role in this transformation. This requires at least two things. On the one hand, it requires the development of an open-minded attitude towards technology and the ability to rethink the profession as we know it today, on the basis of empirical evidence, new ideas and the awareness about the direction that markets, society and technological developments are heading to. On the other, there is urgent need for a research effort directed to anticipating future trends, enabling the sector to prepare for the disruptive changes caused by digital technologies. This inquiry should not be conducted merely from the interpreter's perspective (self-perception, etc.), albeit it remaining a crucial side in the debate, but it should also consider the interests of other stakeholders and encompass considerations of different nature, such as socio-economic parameters.

Even if still marginal in Interpreting Studies, it should be pointed out that the interest for technological matters, especially but not exclusively for RI, as well as the presence of technology in interpreter training are gaining momentum, indicating some degree of awareness is spreading in regards to the importance of technological development to interpreting. This is encouraging. The present book can be considered a small contribution in this direction as it offers some evidence, practical suggestions and new ideas that may help the interpreting community to positively address the upcoming challenges. All its chapters present empirical research in two areas of technological innovation which may have a greater impact on the daily working conditions of interpreters in the immediate future, namely computer-assisted and remote interpreting.

5 Overview of the individual contributions

The book opens with two seminal chapters in the research area around CAI tools and should stimulate scientific and practical discussion on the role of technology use during interpreting. Desmet, Vandierendonck and Defrancq present a pilot study on the potential impact of CAI tools that support the interpretation of numbers. The authors set up a mock-up system to simulate technology that automatically recognizes numbers in the source speech and presents them on a screen in the booth. The study experimentally shows that CAI tools may have the potential to reduce the cognitive load during simultaneous interpreting and improve quality. Considering the quality reached by automatic speech recognition, this study may contribute to a faster adoption of this technology in the interpreting setting.

The issue of finding the right framework to study the impact of CAI tools on the interpreter delivery is pivotal in Prandi's chapter. In her exploratory study, she evaluates the appropriateness of the stimuli adopted for data collection and describes the theoretical framework she chose to conduct the experiment. The final goal of this research project, still underway, is to verify whether the use of CAI tools in the booth causes saturation or, on the contrary, helps prevent it by reducing the cognitive load during terminology search and delivery. The preliminary results derived from the analysis of the test subjects' interpretations seems to indicate that the use of a CAI tool, under specific circumstances, may increase output quality.

Deysel and Lesch focus on CAIT and explore the use of such tools to develop self-assessment skills in the performance of professional interpreters working in the National Parliament of the Republic of South Africa. The research design for this article comprises an evaluation study approach, based on an experimental design that considers the exposure to CAIT for purposes of self-assessment. In order to collect data to address the research questions, a questionnaire, an experiment and interviews were used. The experimental group was exposed to the software *Black Box* in order to measure its impact on the development of their self-assessment skills. The results show that the experimental group of practicing interpreters who were exposed to the software indicated a better understanding of the criteria which are important in the assessment of interpreting performance as well as a greater awareness of the strengths and weaknesses of their performance.

Devaux's chapter explores practicing court interpreters' perceptions of their role in England and Wales when they interpret through videoconferencing systems. The author empirically approaches the subject conducting semi-structured interviews with eighteen participants. The data gathered was analyzed through the innovative theoretical framework of role-space. The results show that the use of technology, unlike in face-to-face court hearings, makes some interpreters perceive their role differently and forces them to create split role models. The use of videoconferencing equipment affects various aspects of their presentation of self, participant alignment, and interaction management. The chapter ends with some recommendations for training court interpreters derived from the experimental results.

Finally, Ziegler and Gigliobianco address the use of remote interpreting in the simultaneous mode. After analyzing the terminological challenges and presenting the basic literature on the topic, they give a detailed overview of the state-of-the art of RI, the technical requirements required for remote interpreting and the relevant international norms. They then introduce a pilot experiment aiming at testing the feasibility of using augmented reality in order to overcome some of the perceived limitations of RI, i.e. exclusion and lack of visuality. The idea of interpreters working and being in control of what the camera(s) show them is certainly attractive and it may trigger research into new interpreting technologies applied to remoteness.

6 Conclusions

There seem to be signs of a new technological breakthrough approaching interpreting, yet not enough research and discussion is devoted to the actual consequences for the profession, both in the short and in the long term. There is an urgent need to understand how technology is disrupting the way interpreters work and to explore the broad terrain of private actions, public policies, and professional dialogue needed to ensure that technological advancements can be shaped to the benefit of interpreters.

It is the hope of the editor that, through this publication, interpreting scholars and professionals will embrace further research and discussions in this exciting area of interpreting studies, exploring new topics at the intersection of technology and interpreting and, in doing so, contributing to preparing the profession to successfully face the upcoming technological turn in interpreting.

References

Andres, Dörte & Stefanie Falk. 2009. Information and communication technologies (ICT) in interpreting: Remote and telephone interpreting. In Dörte Andres & Sonja Pöllabauer (eds.), *Spürst Du wie der Bauch rauf-runter? Fachdolmetschen im Gesundheitsbereich* (InterPartes), 9–27. München: Martin Meidenbauer.

Besnier, Jean-Michel. 2012. *L'homme simplifié: Le syndrome de la touche étoile*. Paris: Fayard.

Causo, José Esteban. 2011. Conference interpreting with information and communication technologies. Experiences from the European Commission DG Interpretation. In Sabine Braun & Judith L. Taylor (eds.), *Videoconference and remote interpreting in criminal proceedings*, 199–203. Guilford: University of Surrey.

Chang, Chia-chien, Michelle Min-chia Wu & Tien-chun Gina Kuo. 2018. Conference interpreting and knowledge acquisition: How professional interpreters tackle unfamiliar topics. *Interpreting* 20(2). 204–231.

Fantinuoli, Claudio. 2017a. Computer-assisted preparation in conference interpreting. *Translation & Interpreting* 9(2). 24–37.

Fantinuoli, Claudio. 2017b. Speech recognition in the interpreter workstation. In *Proceedings of the Translating and the Computer 39 Conference*, 367–377. London: Editions Tradulex.

Fantinuoli, Claudio. 2018a. Computer-assisted interpreting: Challenges and future perspectives. In Gloria Corpas Pastor & Isabel Durán-Muñoz (eds.), *Trends in E-tools and resources for translators and interpreters*, 153–174. Leiden: Brill.

Fantinuoli, Claudio. 2018b. The use of comparable corpora in interpreting practice and teaching. *The Interpreters' Newsletter* 1. 133–149.

Finn, Ed. 2017. *What algorithms want: Imagination in the age of computing*. Cambridge: MIT Press.

Galimberti, Umberto. 2009. *I miti del nostro tempo*. Milano: Feltrinelli.

Gentile, Paola. 2013. The status of conference interpreters: a global survey into the profession. *Rivista internazionale di tecnica della traduzione* 15. 63–82.

Gile, Daniel. 2009. *Basic concepts and models for interpreter and translator training*. Amsterdam/Philadelphia: John Benjamins.

Huws, Ursula. 2016. Logged labour: A new paradigm of work organisation? *Work Organisation, Labour & Globalisation* 10(1). 7–26.

Müller, Markus, Thai Son Nguyen, Jan Niehues, Eunah Cho, Bastian Krüger, Thanh-Le Ha, Kevin Kilgour, Matthias Sperber, Mohammed Mediani, Sebastian Stüker & Alex Waibel. 2016. Lecture Translator: Speech translation framework for simultaneous lecture translation. In, 82–86. Association for Computational Linguistics.

Neufeind, Max, Jacqueline O'Reilly & Florian Ranft (eds.). 2018. *Work in the digital age: Challenges of the fourth industrial revolution.* Lanham: Policy Network.

Pernice, Kara. 2017. *F-shaped pattern of reading on the web: Misunderstood, but still relevant (even on mobile).* Tech. rep. https://www.nngroup.com/articles/f-shaped-pattern-reading-web-content/.

Pym, Anthony. 2011. What technology does to translating. *Translation & Interpreting* 3(1). 1–9.

Ross, Bella, Ekaterina Pechenkina, Carol Aeschliman & Anne-Marie Chase. 2017. Print versus digital texts: Understanding the experimental research and challenging the dichotomies. *Research in Learning Technology* 25(0).

Stewart, Craig, Nikolai Vogler, Junjie Hu, Jordan Boyd-Graber & Graham Neubig. 2018. Automatic estimation of simultaneous interpreter performance. In *Proceedings of the 56th annual meeting of the association for computational linguistics,* 662–666.

Takeda, Kayoko & Jesús Baigorri Jalón (eds.). 2016. *New insights in the history of interpreting.* Amsterdam/Philadelphia: John Benjamins.

Xu, Ran. 2018. Corpus-based terminological preparation for simultaneous interpreting. *Interpreting* 20(1). 29–58.

Zanettin, Federico. 2002. Corpora in translation practice. In *Proceedings of the Workshop Language Resources for Translation Work and Research,* 10–14.

Chapter 2

Simultaneous interpretation of numbers and the impact of technological support

Bart Desmet
University of Ghent

Mieke Vandierendonck
University of Ghent

Bart Defrancq
University of Ghent

> In simultaneous interpretation, numbers are a common source of errors. They are often characterized by low predictability from the context and high information density, and the interpreter is therefore required to change strategies with respect to listening, memory and production. Booth technology that automatically recognizes numbers in the source speech and presents them on a screen could reduce the cognitive load and improve translation quality.
>
> In this chapter, we present an experimental study on the properties of numbers that make them more or less challenging for the interpreter, and provide some evidence on how a technological support system influences performance.

1 Introduction

Translation and interpreting are often called sister disciplines, but the integration of the respective activities with technology could not be more different. Computer-assisted translation is now standard practice and machine translation has become so successful that it now seems plausible to some that translators will devote most of their time to post-editing in the near future. In interpreting, by contrast, technological support is scarce, except for electronic devices used for

Bart Desmet, Mieke Vandierendonck & Bart Defrancq. 2018. Simultaneous interpretation of numbers and the impact of technological support. In Claudio Fantinuoli (ed.), *Interpreting and technology*, 13–27. Berlin: Language Science Press. DOI:10.5281/zenodo.1493291

terminology support in the booth (Fantinuoli 2012) or for taking notes in consecutive interpreting and hybrid modes (Orlando 2014; 2016; Goldsmith 2017). There are a number of reasons for this discrepancy. First, in the area of interpreting, technology and, in particular, natural language technologies, are far less developed than in the area of translation. In fact, automated interpreting systems that are claimed to be effective (such as the Google Pixel Buds) first transform spoken language into some form of written or digital code before translating and converting it back to a spoken form. Automatic interpreting therefore depends on advances made on the translation front and on the availability of accurate speech-to-text and text-to-speech software. Second, spoken language does not come in nicely packed grammatical sentences but is rife with hesitations, unfinished sequences, repairs, etc., which are much harder to handle for an automatic translation system than for a human brain. Replacing the human interpreter with a reliable automatic one will require additional progress in the analysis of human language in context. Finally, even technology-supported human interpreting develops slowly, as there is little agreement among scholars whether additional sources of information in the booth are really helpful or rather distracting for the interpreter. There is also evidence of a certain aversion to technology among interpreters (Corpas Pastor & Fern 2016), which is likely to delay the adoption and use of technological support for some time.

The slow progress of technology in interpreting is due to its own set of challenges. Simultaneous interpreting is a cognitively demanding task consisting of a variety of processing tasks which have to be carried out in parallel (Gile 1995; Seeber 2011). Some sub-tasks are felt by most interpreters to be particularly challenging: the interpretation of numbers, of names, of enumerations, etc. (Gile 2009). This paper will focus on numbers and on the effects of (simulated) technological support for the interpretation of numbers. The main research question is whether displaying numbers on a screen in the conference room, immediately after they have been articulated by the speaker, increases the accuracy of numbers in the target text. This experimental pilot study thus aims to determine if limited technological support, which would consist of automatic number recognition in the source text and the display of a numerical transcription, is at all helpful in interpreting.

2 Numbers in interpreting

There is a very broad consensus among interpreters that numbers are particularly difficult to interpret. Yet, research on the topic of interpreting numbers is rather limited (Mead 2015: 287). Starting with Braun & Clarici (1996), several experimental studies have been conducted on the success rate of number rendition in interpreting, showing that overall performance is relatively poor, both in professionals and in student interpreters. In Braun & Clarici (1996), for instance, 12 students obtained a mean error score of close to 70% while simultaneously interpreting numbers contained in speeches. Mazza (2001) reports slightly better performances by 15 students, but the mean error rate in her study is still in the 45–50% range. The findings of Pinochi (2009), based on interpretations by 16 students, are fairly consistent with Mazza's result. Pinochi compares interpretations from two different source languages (English and German) into one target language and finds that error rates are nearly identical (ca. 40%), even though interpreters have to overcome additional challenges due to differences in the syntax of numbers between German and Italian.

Korpal (2016) compares student performances with performances by professional interpreters for slow and fast delivery rates. He finds that, although professionals obtain lower error rates than students, nearly 30% of numbers in the interpretation are either wrong or absent altogether in the slower delivery rate. The error rate jumps to 43% for the highest delivery rate. Among students, error rates are in line with Mazza's findings: 44% for the slow delivery rate and 56% for the fast one. Timarová's experimental study of 28 professional interpreters yields an error rate for numbers of approximately 40% (Timarová 2012). In a corpus study reported in Collard & Defrancq (2017), error rates for numbers in interpretations collected in the European Parliament are close to 18%. One possible, but unverifiable, explanation for the discrepancy between the experimental and the corpus results is the presence of a booth colleague who takes down the numbers for the interpreter ensuring the turn. The numbers can then simply be read off the notebook. In an experimental setting, interpreters perform in isolation, and even though they are usually allowed to take down numbers themselves, this is obviously more difficult than when assistance is provided by a colleague in the booth. In any case, even in naturalistic data, close to one out of five numbers of the source text is rendered incorrectly or omitted in the target language. Based on this data, technological support could be helpful in the booth, and it has the potential to reduce the number of errors and omissions.

Scholars have identified several reasons why interpreting numbers is a challenge. Numbers lack a conceptual representation (Timarová 2012; Seeber 2015) and are, therefore, not embedded in a conceptual structure allowing interpreters to anticipate them. This lack of predictability of numbers is widely recognised as an obstacle to their interpretation (Braun & Clarici 1996; Mazza 2001; Pinochi 2009; Mead 2015). Numbers are highly informative (Alessandrini 1990), as every component of a number is a meaningful unit representing only one particular meaning. This prevents interpreters from using strategies such as paraphrasing or reformulation (Pinochi 2009). Numbers also usually lack redundant material, which makes them more informative (Gile 1995; Seeber 2015). Source texts with high information density are known to increase cognitive load in interpreters. As hypothesized by Pinochi (2009), differences in number syntax between source and target language can exacerbate this load, as interpreters not only have to render each numeral unit correctly but also swap the order of some of the units (e.g. between English and German).

One of the universally recommended strategies is note-taking (Setton 1999; Jones 2002; Mead 2015): interpreters are advised to stop the delivery of the target text as soon as they hear a number, write it down on a notepad in the booth and read it off while starting up the delivery again. The findings of Mazza (2001) seem to support the hypothesis that interpreting is more accurate in cases where interpreters jotted down the number. Without a notepad, shortening the ear-voice span (EVS) and changing the listening strategy seem to be the most effective coping strategies: Setton (1999), for instance, observes that errors typically occur when the EVS is more than 3–4 seconds. Following Seleskovitch (1975), Pinochi (2009) advocates a switch from intelligent hearing, i.e. taking into account the context to draw inferences, to literal hearing, i.e. paying attention to the item in isolation.

Assistance by the booth colleague in writing down numbers and visual input provided by the speakers, such as a copy of the speech to be used in the booth, or the projected presentation slides, are said to be beneficial (Mead 2015). Lamberger-Felber (2001) reports a significant increase of number and name accuracy (53% to 68% fewer errors, depending on the source speech) in an experiment when interpreters are provided the text of the speech in the booth, compared to when they do not have the text at their disposal. Accuracy is highest when, in addition, they are given time to prepare the text they are supplied with. It is to be noted, however, that this is the combined accuracy for numbers and names together. Even for the condition without text, high accuracy rates are obtained (mean of 85.7%). This seems to suggest that names cause significantly fewer problems in simultaneous interpreting than numbers.

While assistance and visual input are likely to boost performance, they are beyond the control of the interpreter. Technological support could solve that problem: if interpreters could rely on technology that systematically displays numbers as they are pronounced, it could improve the accuracy of the numbers they deliver. Currently, limited applications exist in conference rooms with voting systems, where the results of votes are displayed on a screen in the booth, but the targeted use of natural language processing applications could make it possible in the near future to extract numerical information from online speeches.

3 Technology in interpreting

Technology has always been essential to simultaneous interpreting, with audio equipment and booth consoles providing the communication backbone for it to occur. More recently, remote interpreting has been making forays into the profession. Fantinuoli (2018) categorizes these technologies as primarily setting-oriented, since they determine the external conditions in which interpreting takes place. Process-oriented technologies, on the other hand, are designed to support the interpreter in the various phases and processes of interpreting itself, e.g. for the acquisition, organization and retrieval of information, both before and during an assignment. Such technologies aim to directly influence the interpreting process, its associated cognitive load and the quality of its outcome. As such, they are the defining components of computer-assisted interpreting (CAI).

Currently, existing CAI tools are mostly focused on terminological support, whether in preparing for an assignment or for access in the booth. This focus is not surprising as domain-specific terms are an important obstacle to interpreting quality, and CAI tools have the potential of helping interpreters use them more accurately and consistently. Recent studies (Will 2015; Fantinuoli 2017a; Costa et al. 2018) have surveyed existing CAI tools for terminology management, and determined relevant criteria to evaluate them. For a knowledge management tool to be practical in the booth, an important requirement is that it allows the interpreter to access reference material quickly and with as little additional cognitive load as possible. This can be achieved with good knowledge representation, clear presentation and ergonomic operation, and good search algorithms.

It is essential that relevant information can be retrieved fast, i.e. within the ear-voice span. Automatic Speech Recognition (ASR) has the potential of speeding up the look-up process and solving the cognitive effort and latency of manual querying. Technological advances in the field have been rapid in recent years, especially since the introduction of neural networks (Yu & Deng 2016). Given the current state of the art in ASR and its foreseeable progress, it seems to be a matter of time before this technology is used in CAI tools to support interpreters with terminology look-up, and/or with information-dense content like numbers, as explored in Fantinuoli (2017b). This paper will focus on the latter of these aspects.

While the development and adoption of CAI tools has been limited, scientific research on the impact of their use has been even scarcer. The main contribution of this work is that it experimentally evaluates the potential impact of ASR-driven CAI support that displays numbers on-screen in real time.

4 Experiment

The aim of this experiment is twofold: to determine if limited technological support can improve the accuracy of interpreted numbers, and how this improvement breaks down over different number and error types. In the following sections, we describe the system used as a proxy for automatic number support, the participants, selected speeches and the distribution of numbers in them, the experimental setup and the evaluation parameters.

4.1 A proxy system for automatic number support

An ideal system for number support during simultaneous interpretation would consist of three components:

1. ASR that can transform an incoming speech signal into text quickly, accurately and without the need for being tuned to a specific speaker or accent

2. software to isolate numbers from the text in meaningful units

3. a way of ergonomically presenting those numbers to the interpreter

Since no such system existed at the time this study was conducted, a mock-up system was used to simulate the desired behavior. Microsoft PowerPoint presentations were prepared ahead of time based on the speech transcripts, containing one slide per number in the speech. Figure 1 shows an example slide as used in the experiment. Numbers were presented in a numerical format with spacing between multiples of a thousand, and formatted in a large fixed-width font. The two previous numbers, if available, were displayed above the focus number, so that numbers in rapid succession would stay accessible longer. During the experiment, the presentation was shown on a big screen in the conference room, and slides were manually advanced immediately after a number had been fully pronounced, i.e. simulating an automatic system with minimal latency.

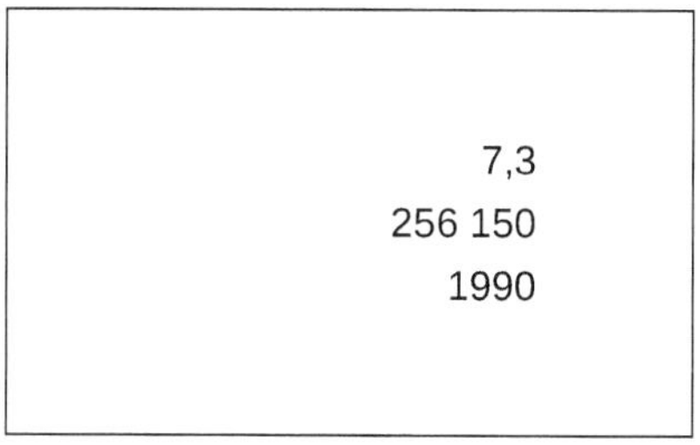

```
          7,3
        256 150
          1990
```

Figure 1: Example of the mock-up technological support, showing the three most recent numbers that have been pronounced by the speaker (Microsoft PowerPoint slide). New numbers are added to the bottom of the slide, with old numbers shifting upwards. A maximum of three numbers is shown.

4.2 Participants

The experiment was performed with ten interpretation students enrolled in the postgraduate program for Conference Interpreting at Ghent University with Dutch as an A-language. Seven of them had completed a 4-year applied linguistics program with a focus on French, the three others with a focus on German, making them proficient at the C2 level according to the CEFR framework (Council of Europe 2001). At the time of the experiment, all participants had received 5 weeks of simultaneous training at the postgraduate level and were taking additional *retour* classes for the source languages of the experiment. They were all graduates of a master program in interpreting that offers an introduction to simultaneous interpreting and limited practice. Participants were aged between 22 and 27 years and 9 of them were female.

4.3 Speeches

Four experimental speeches of similar difficulty and length were prepared, with parallel versions in French and German. The average text length for French was 1121 words, the German texts conveyed the same content with almost 10% fewer words, at an average of 1022 per text. German compounds are written as a single word, which largely explains this discrepancy. The texts dealt with diverse topics (Amazon, child labour, inheritance law and natural disasters), and specific terminology was provided to the participants before the start of each speech.

Like in the experiments of Braun & Clarici (1996) and Mazza (2001), the start of each speech (150 words) contained no numbers, to allow participants to get accustomed to the experimental conditions. After that, 20 numbers occurred at random intervals. They were equally distributed over four categories, with each text containing exactly 5 instances of each category: simple whole numbers (e.g. 87 or 60 000), complex whole numbers (e.g. 387 or 65 400), decimals (e.g. 28.3) and years (e.g. 2012). We distinguished between simple and complex whole numbers based on the number of meaningful units rather than the number of digits, since large numbers can be conceptually simple (e.g. 1 million contains only 2 meaningful units). In this study, numbers containing 3 or more meaningful units were considered complex.

4.4 Setup

Participants were required to interpret into their A-language: Dutch. The experiment was conducted in two sessions: one for French with 7 participants, and one for German with 3 participants. There was no overlap between the two participant groups. Offering two source languages created an opportunity to check the results for the influence of number syntax: German and Dutch are both "unit-decade" languages (61 is *eenenzestig* in Dutch: 'one-and-sixty'), whereas French is a "decade-unit" language (*soixante-et-un* 'sixty and one'). In interpreting from French into Dutch, the order of certain units inside the number needs to be changed, whereas if German is the source language, no such changes are required.

Before the experiment, participants were informed that numbers would occur with high frequency in the speeches, and they were familiarized with the mock-up technological support. Each speech was then read by a near-native, and recorded digitally, along with all interpretations into Dutch. The first two texts were interpreted without simulated technological support, whereas it was available for the last two. The rate of delivery, a potential problem trigger for interpretation quality (Gile 1995), was within the optimal range for interpreters: an average of 121 words per minute for French, and 101 words per minute for German. This difference in rate can be partly explained by the higher information density of German words, but the German speaker also took more time to deliver speeches with identical content to their French counterparts: an average of 608 seconds, 9.4% longer than the 556 seconds for French. Within the same language, the delivery rate for speeches interpreted without technological support was slightly slower than those interpreted with support: an average of 115 and 128 words per minute for French, and 100 and 102 words per minute for German, respectively. Any benefits from the technological support can therefore not be attributed to a slower rate of delivery.

After the experiment, a questionnaire polled whether the participants had found the technological support helpful or distracting, how long it took to get used to it, and what they would change about it.

4.5 Evaluation

Given the focus of this study on interpreting numbers, the recordings were analyzed to produce systematic records for each number. These include a transcript of the number stimulus in the source speech and the provided interpretation, which allows the performance to be coded: has the number been interpreted correctly, and if not, what kind of error was made? For the categorization of errors, we follow Pinochi (2009), which in turn was adapted from Braun & Clarici (1996):

Omission: the number is missing or has been replaced by a general expression (e.g. *47* becomes *many*).

Approximation: the order of magnitude is correct, but the number has been rounded up or down (e.g. *47* becomes *around 50*). These adaptations can be viewed as interpretation tactics rather than mistakes.

Lexical mistakes: the order of magnitude of the number is correct, but some of its components have been changed (e.g. *47* becomes *49*).

Transposition: all components are correct, but their order has been changed (e.g. *47* becomes *74*). This error can be especially frequent when the source and target language use a different number syntax (pronouncing units or tens first).

Syntactic mistakes: the order of magnitude is incorrect, even though the right components may be present (e.g. *47* becomes *470*).

Phonological mistakes: the error can be explained by phonological confusion in the source stimulus (e.g. *14* becomes *40*, a near-homophone in English).

Other mistakes: miscellaneous errors that do not fit any of the other categories, or numbers that combine multiple error types (e.g. *47* becomes *740*).

Additionally, the records contain information on the source language, source speech, participant, the type of number, and whether the experimental technological support was available (i.e., the independent variable). These variables allow the impact of CAI support to be analyzed from multiple perspectives, as presented in the following section.

5 Results and discussion

The experiment yielded 40 recordings of 4 speeches interpreted by 10 participants. French was the source language in 28 of them, German in 12, and half of them were interpreted with technological support for numbers. With 20 numbers per recording, a total of 800 observations was available for this pilot study.

5.1 The impact of technological support for interpreting numbers

Numbers are difficult to interpret, as the experimental results show. The average accuracy on numbers in the control setting, without technological support, was 56.5% over all test subjects and languages, i.e. an average error rate of 43.5%. The observed performances were thus completely in line with the 40–50% error rate found in most other studies. Accuracy between individuals varied from 27.5% to 90%, and the interpretations from German were more accurate on average (74% vs 49%). This could be due to the higher similarity between the German and Dutch number systems, but the number of participants is too small to rule out individual differences as the main cause of this divergence. Another explanation is the slower rate of delivery for German than for French.

When technological support was made available, the performance on numbers improved dramatically. Average accuracy rose by 30 percentage points to 86.5%, and the absolute number of errors dropped from 174 to 54 out of 400, an error reduction of 69%. This finding was fairly consistent with the 53–68% decrease reported by Lamberger-Felber (2001) for numbers and names, when copies of speeches were made available to the interpreter. A paired t-test showed that the performance difference was highly significant for both source languages ($p < 0.001$). It should not come as a surprise that individuals that scored poorly without support benefit most from having it, at least in absolute terms of avoided errors (up to 21 fewer errors on 40 numbers). Interestingly, relative error reduction was moderate (43%) to high (90%) regardless of a subject's performance in the control setting. In other words, even if an interpreter was highly competent at conveying numbers without support, he or she was able to reduce their error rate significantly when support is available.

It is obvious from these results that CAI support for numbers has the potential of drastically reducing errors on numbers. Nevertheless, it needs to be emphasized that these results indicate the ceiling performance of what can be achieved with technological support, or with a dedicated booth mate, for that matter. The tested mock-up system has a minimal delay and its output is entirely accurate. With such a reliable system, the interpreter can choose to reduce the listening and memory efforts to focus more on production. Further research is required to test how an imperfect output would affect the distribution of effort.

Feedback from the questionnaires indicated that all participants perceived the support as helpful. Three participants reported that it took some time to get used to the system, while for the others the transition was almost immediate. Two respondents were sometimes distracted by the system because it focused their attention on numbers at the expense of other content. Future evaluations should elucidate if distraction can be reduced with increased familiarity with number support, or different ways of providing it. Specifically, adding units (e.g. *km* or *percent*) or concepts to the numbers could be beneficial to recall their usage in context, although this may require cues that are specific to the source language.

5.2 The influence of number type

The numbers expressed in the experimental speeches were balanced over four categories: simple and complex whole numbers, decimals and dates. Figure 2 shows the performance in terms of accuracy, categorized by these number types.

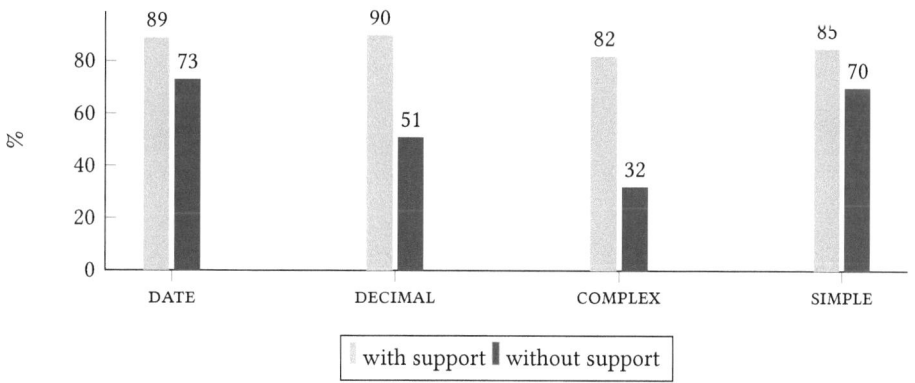

Figure 2: Average accuracy per number type in both experimental conditions

It can be observed that in the standard setting without support, interpreters experience most difficulties with complex and decimal numbers. Accuracy rates for these types are low at 32% and 51%, respectively, compared to around 70% for both simple numbers and dates. These results corroborate previous findings. This study used the same number typology as Mazza (2001), with the exception that we distinguish whole numbers based on complexity rather than size; Pinochi (2009) separates whole numbers into three categories, based on the complexity of pronouncing them. In all three studies, large or complex whole numbers are found to cause the most errors, followed by decimals, and small or simple whole numbers and dates are the easiest to interpret.

When interpreters have access to technological support, the differences in error rate per number type almost disappear. Overall, we see that each type benefits from it. As expected, the largest gain is for complex whole and decimal numbers, with absolute error reductions of 50 and 39%, respectively (significant at $p < 0.01$). Even for the simpler number categories there are significant improvements ($p < 0.05$). With technological support, accuracy is almost identical across number types, which suggests that the remaining errors are due to factors other than the complexity of the number. A detailed analysis of the remaining errors is still to be made.

5.3 Error type analysis

A total of 228 errors was observed in the experiment. Figure 3 presents them separated by type.

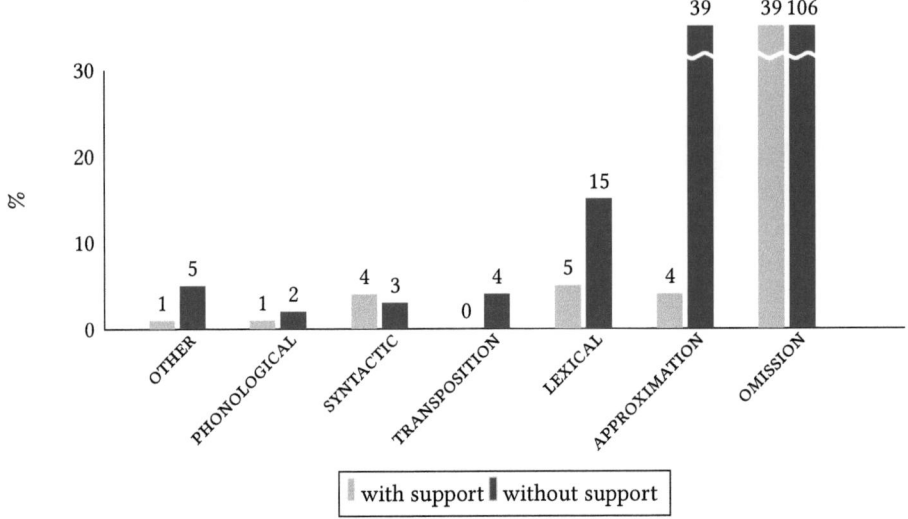

Figure 3: Error count per type in both experimental conditions

By far the most frequently occurring error is omission, regardless of the availability of technological support. Technological support significantly reduces the number of omissions ($p < 0.05$), but omissions remain frequent and their relative weight in the total error load increases from 61 to 72%. We see two possible explanations for this. Some numbers come in information-dense sections of a speech, and omitting them may be a necessity to limit cognitive load or to avoid increasing EVS. In such cases, even having the number available on screen would not help in reproducing it in context. Second, it could be that technological support causes complacency or confusion when numbers are heard. If an interpreter reduces the listening effort and relies on a support system to receive the number, adequate context may be lacking to convey its meaning.

Approximations are often used in the control setting, but only when the source stimulus was a decimal or a complex whole number. Approximating is a useful strategy when numbers have not been entirely understood, or when they are too large to fit in working memory. With the addition of technological support, this strategy is used almost 10 times less often, since the tasks of comprehension and working memory are effectively solved. The error reduction is significant at $p < 0.001$.

Lexical mistakes, the third most frequent error in the control setting, occur three times less often when support is available. The other four error categories do not occur frequently in either of the settings. Differences between the two experimental settings are not significant or lack support.

The error distributions are in line with the findings of Mazza (2001) and Pinochi (2009), who also found omissions and approximations to be most frequent, in that order.

6 Conclusions and future work

This paper presented an experimental pilot study of the potential impact of booth technology that supports the interpretation of numbers. Our mock-up system simulates technology that automatically recognizes numbers in the source speech and presents them on a screen in the conference room, in order to reduce the cognitive load and improve translation quality.

Technological support improves overall accuracy on numbers from 56.5 to 86.5 percent, reducing the amount of errors by two thirds. The improvement is statistically significant for all participants. Technological help is most helpful in reducing errors on complex numbers and decimals, the two categories that are most often interpreted incorrectly. Omissions are the most frequent error, followed by approximations. The occurrence of the latter drops by almost 90 percent when support is available.

Since the experiment was performed with students, the results are not readily applicable to professional interpreters. Even though the outcome of the experiment clearly shows the potential of CAI support for numbers, it must be emphasized that our experimental design is not based on automatic recognition of numbers in speech. Automatic Speech Recognition might not achieve perfect recognition and minimal latency. Therefore, our results describe the ceiling performance that could be achieved with such an ideal system. Further studies should be carried out on how interpreters deal with discrepancies between auditory input from a speaker and visual input from an automatic recognition system, increased delay or different modes of presentation. Further research should also focus on the rendition of items used in combination with numbers, as it is known that interpreters tend to direct so many of their attentional resources to numbers that errors also frequently occur in the context of numbers (Gile 2009).

References

Alessandrini, Maria Serena. 1990. Translating numbers in consecutive interpretation: An experimental study. *The Interpreters' Newsletter* 3. 77–80.

Braun, Sabine & Andrea Clarici. 1996. Inaccuracy for numerals in simultaneous interpretation: Neurolinguistic and neuropsychological perspectives. *The Interpreters' Newsletter* 7. 85–102.

Collard, Camille & Bart Defrancq. 2017. Sex differences in simultaneous interpreting: A corpus-based study. Poster presented at the CIUTI Forum 2017, Geneva.

Corpas Pastor, Gloria & Lily May Fern. 2016. *A survey of interpreters' needs and practices related to language technology*. Tech. rep. Málaga: University of Málaga.

Costa, Hernani, Gloria Corpas Pastor & Isabel Durán-Muñoz. 2018. Assessing terminology management systems for interpreters. In Gloria Corpas Pastor & Isabel Durán-Muñoz (eds.), *Trends in E-tools and resources for translators and interpreters*, 57–84. Leiden: Brill.

Council of Europe. 2001. *Common European framework of reference for languages: Learning, teaching, assessment*. Cambridge: Press Syndicate of the University of Cambridge.

Fantinuoli, Claudio. 2012. *Design and implementation of a terminology and knowledge management software for conference interpreter*. Mainz dissertation.

Fantinuoli, Claudio. 2017a. Computer-assisted preparation in conference interpreting. *Translation & Interpreting* 9(2). 24–37.

Fantinuoli, Claudio. 2017b. Speech recognition in the interpreter workstation. In *Proceedings of the Translating and the Computer 39 Conference*, 367–377. London: Editions Tradulex.

Fantinuoli, Claudio. 2018. Computer-assisted interpreting: Challenges and future perspectives. In Gloria Corpas Pastor & Isabel Durán-Muñoz (eds.), *Trends in E-tools and resources for translators and interpreters*, 153–174. Leiden: Brill.

Gile, Daniel. 1995. *Basic concepts and models for interpreter and translator training*. Amsterdam/Philadelphia: John Benjamins.

Gile, Daniel. 2009. *Basic concepts and models for interpreter and translator training*. Amsterdam/Philadelphia: John Benjamins.

Goldsmith, Josh. 2017. A comparative user evaluation of tablets and tools for consecutive interpreters. *Proceedings of Translating and the Computer* 39. 40–50.

Jones, Roderick. 2002. *Conference interpreting explained*. Abingdon/New York: Routledge.

Korpal, Pawel. 2016. *Linguistic and psychological indicators of stress in simultaneous interpreting*. Poznan dissertation.

Lamberger-Felber, Heike. 2001. Text-oriented research into interpreting: Examples from a case-study. *Hermes* 26. 39–63.

Mazza, Cristina. 2001. Numbers in simultaneous interpretation. *The Interpreters' Newsletter* 11. 87–104.

Mead, Peter. 2015. Numbers. In Franz Pöchhacker (ed.), *Routledge encyclopedia of interpreting studies*, 286–288. Abingdon/New York: Routledge.

Orlando, Mark. 2014. A study on the amenability of digital pen technology in a hybrid mode of interpreting: Consec-simul with notes. *Translation & Interpreting* 6(2). 39–54.

Orlando, Mark. 2016. *Training 21st century translators and interpreters: At the crossroads of practice, research and pedagogy*. Berlin: Timme.

Pinochi, Diletta. 2009. Simultaneous interpretation of numbers: Comparing German and English to Italian. An experimental study. *The Interpreters' Newsletter* 14. 33–57.

Seeber, Kilian G. 2011. Cognitive load in simultaneous interpreting: Existing theories – new models. *Interpreting* 13(2). 176–204.

Seeber, Kilian G. 2015. Simultaneous interpreting. In Holly Mikkelson & Renée Jourdenais (eds.), *The Routledge handbook of interpreting*. Abingdon/New York: Routledge.

Seleskovitch, Danica. 1975. *Langage, langue et mémoire. Etude de la prise de notes en interpretation consécutive*. Paris.

Setton, Robin. 1999. *Simultaneous interpretation: A cognitive-pragmatic analysis*. Amsterdam/Philadelphia: John Benjamins.

Timarová, Šárka. 2012. *Working memory in simultaneous interpreting*. Antwerp dissertation.

Will, Martin. 2015. Zur Eignung simultanfähiger Terminologiesysteme für das Konferenzdolmetschen. *Zeitschrift für Translationswissenschaft und Fachkommunikation* 8(1). 179–201.

Yu, Dong & Li Deng. 2016. *Automatic speech recognition: A deep learning approach*. London: Springer.

Chapter 3

An exploratory study on CAI tools in simultaneous interpreting: Theoretical framework and stimulus validation

Bianca Prandi
University of Mainz

> The acquisition of terminology and specialized knowledge prior to a technical conference represents a fundamental phase in the interpreter's workflow, but quick and easy access to terminological information during the interpreting task is equally important to support the interpreter in the rendition of terminology and to ensure a high-quality interpreting performance.
>
> Over the past few years, terminology management tools have been developed specifically for interpreters, but the impact of such tools on the cognitive processes involved in simultaneous interpreting is still unclear. To this end, an exploratory study was conducted to evaluaonference interpreters were covered.te the appropriateness of the stimuli adopted for data collection and to verify whether the use of computer-assisted interpreting tools causes saturation or, on the contrary, helps prevent it by reducing the local cognitive load during terminology search and delivery of the target text.

1 Introduction

Computer-assisted interpreting (CAI) emerged around 10 years ago to provide interpreters with tools to prepare for specialized events and to support them along the individual phases of their workflow, from preparation, to interpretation proper, to follow-up work after the assignment. CAI tools thus rationalize the interpreter's terminology work by making preparation more efficient and ultimately aim at improving the quality of the interpreter's output, at least in terms

Bianca Prandi. 2018. An exploratory study on CAI tools in simultaneous interpreting: Theoretical framework and stimulus validation. In Claudio Fantinuoli (ed.), *Interpreting and technology*, 29–59. Berlin: Language Science Press. DOI:10.5281/zenodo.1493293

of terminological precision and adequacy. Rütten (2007) and Will (2009) developed a theoretical model of the interpreter's preparation work and laid the foundations for how a CAI tool should be structured in order to address the specific needs of conference interpreters, which are mainly linked to the online nature of interpreting and the time constraints it entails.

To date, the number of CAI tools available to interpreters is limited and their functionalities do not always cover all the phases of the interpreting process. Fantinuoli (2018) distinguishes between first-generation and second-generation CAI tools. The first (e.g. Interplex[1] and Terminus[2]) are "designed to manage multilingual glossaries in an interpreter-friendly manner" (Fantinuoli 2018: 164), but do not offer an advanced search algorithm. The latter "offer advanced functionalities that go beyond basic terminology management, such as features to organize textual material, retrieve information from corpora or other resources, learn conceptualized domains, and advanced search functions" (Fantinuoli 2018: 164) and include Intragloss[3] and InterpretBank[4]. Interpreter's Help[5] can also be considered a second-generation CAI tool, as it implements an advanced search function through its companion tool Boothmate[6].

Following the recent introduction of these tools on the market, first attempts at an evaluation have been made. Two main trends can be identified in this respect. The most recent one focuses on developing a set of criteria against which the tools can be evaluated (Costa et al. 2018; Will 2015). This approach is certainly ambitious, but it remains somewhat arbitrary. The evaluation criteria mainly reflect the features offered by the tools, but do not consider how they influence the product of the interpreting process in terms of terminological quality and whether they optimize the interpreters' preparation and facilitate their work in the booth, by making the online retrieval of terminological units easier and improving the terminological quality. While the number and type of features of CAI tools certainly is of interest for practitioners, the main reason for choosing to use CAI tools, and to prefer one tool to the other ones available, should be the ability of such tools to positively influence the interpreter's work in terms of cognitive capacity and, ultimately, quality.

This is where the second trend in the evaluation of CAI tools comes into play. Soon after the development of the first CAI tools, the first studies on the topic ap-

---

[1] http://www.fourwillows.com/interplex.html
[2] http://www.wintringham.ch/cgi/ayawp.pl?T=terminus
[3] http://intragloss.com
[4] http://www.interpretbank.com
[5] https://interpretershelp.com
[6] https://interpretershelp.com/boothmate

peared. Apart from a few Master's theses, which are limited in scope and often take a descriptive approach rather than an investigative one (see for example De Merulis 2013), a rather small number of publications can be found which mostly deal with the application of CAI tools to the preparation phase (Xu 2018; Fantinuoli 2017a). When it comes to the use of CAI tools in the booth, the number of studies is very limited, as is their scope. First attempts at an empirical analysis of the use of CAI tools during simultaneous interpreting (SI) can be identified in Prandi (2015a,b) and Biagini (2015). These initial investigations of the issue speak in favor of the usability of CAI tools and seem to suggest that they do improve the terminological quality of SI. Both experiments were based on a product-oriented analysis of the test subjects' deliveries. Biagini also included a statistical analysis of transcription data. Apart from these initial analyses, no empirical methodology has been tested in a wide-ranging experiment which implements psycho-physiological, process-oriented methods in addition to product-based analysis. Moreover, Fantinuoli (2017b) recently addressed the topic of the integration of automatic speech recognition (ASR) in CAI tools for use in the booth.

A PhD research project underway at the Johannes Gutenberg University of Mainz/Germersheim (Prandi 2016; 2017b,a) aims at bridging this research gap. By triangulating eye-tracking data and the analysis of the test subjects' transcriptions, the project aims at providing a picture not only of the usability of CAI tools during simultaneous interpreting, but also of the local variations in Cognitive Load (CL) and of the terminological quality of simultaneous interpretation performed with the support of a CAI tool when compared to more traditional terminology management solutions. Through the study, I hope to develop a research methodology that can be used to evaluate CAI tools and provide the much-needed empirical data that will be helpful not only to practitioners in choosing the best tool, but also to software developers, by highlighting potential shortcomings.

After discussing the theoretical framework of my analysis (§2), I present the research desiderata and the structure of an exploratory study conducted to test my research methodology (§3). §4 describes the rationale behind the stimuli used in the experiment and the features of the speeches used. I then present the results of the analysis of the transcriptions (§5), which I use to evaluate the appropriateness of the stimuli. In the conclusions, I address future work and provide suggestions for further research.

2 Theoretical framework

In the investigation of simultaneous interpreting performed with the support of CAI tools, my aim is not only to look at the product of such activity, but also at the process that lies behind it. For this reason, in establishing a theoretical framework for my analysis, I took into consideration the two theoretical models that set out to describe interpreting from a procedural point of view and that address the allocation of cognitive resources during this very complex mental activity: Gile's Effort Model (EM) and Seeber's Cognitive Load Model (CLM) of simultaneous interpreting. In this section, I discuss why Seeber's approach is more suited to the operationalization of my hypotheses.

2.1 Gile's Effort Model and Seeber's Cognitive Load Model of simultaneous interpreting

The main point of divergence between Gile's Effort Model (Gile 1988; 1997; 1999) and Seeber's Cognitive Load Model lies in the theoretical assumptions they stem from. Gile draws from Kahneman's single resource theory (Kahneman 1973) which does not find much validation in scientific literature. If there is one single pool of resources interpreters can adopt, how can some interpreters perform a terminological search on the Internet, while at the same time delivering a perfectly acceptable rendition of the original speech? This kind of multi-tasking might seem impossible to a first-year interpreter trainee, but is commonly observed among experienced professional interpreters. The second controversial assumption is that interpreters work close to saturation level most of the time (Gile's "tightrope hypothesis", 1999). While this might be true in some cases, for instance when the source speech is particularly dense, fast, or pronounced with a non-native accent, there might very well be cases in which the interpreter has enough spare cognitive resources to do something else while interpreting.

In his Cognitive Load Model of simultaneous interpreting, Seeber takes an opposite approach to Gile's, basing his model on Wickens's multiple resource theory and on his Cognitive Load Model (1984; 2002). Wickens developed his model to account for the fact that qualitative differences in tasks being performed at the same time lead to "differences in time-sharing efficiency" (Wickens 2002: 162), as shown by Kantowitz & Knight (1976) and Wickens (1976) himself. According to Wickens, different kinds of tasks require resources that are managed by discrete structures. When two or more tasks are performed simultaneously and "all other things [are] equal (i.e. equal resource demand or single task difficulty), two tasks that both demand one level of a given dimension (e.g. two tasks demanding visual perception) will interfere with each other more than two tasks that demand separate levels of the dimension (e.g. one visual, one auditory task)" (Wickens 2002). In other words, performing a visual and an auditory task simultaneously will be "easier" (i.e. more efficient), because the underlying structures are not shared, than performing two visual tasks, as they share the same structures. In his model, Wickens identifies four dimensions, each made up of two "levels":

- processing stages (perception & cognition[7]/responding)
- processing codes (spatial/verbal)
- processing modalities (visual/auditory)
- visual processing (ambient/focal)

Not shown in the graphic representation of the model (Figure 1), but postulated by Wickens, is an additional pool of general capacity, which is always available to all tasks. In his adaptation of Wickens's model to simultaneous interpreting, Seeber takes a step further, simplifying the graphical representation of Wickens's model by turning it into a 2D model (see Figure 2). This has two main advantages. First, it allows seeing all "sides" of the cube (i.e. all dimensions) at once. Second, it graphically introduces the general capacity left out in Wickens's "cube".

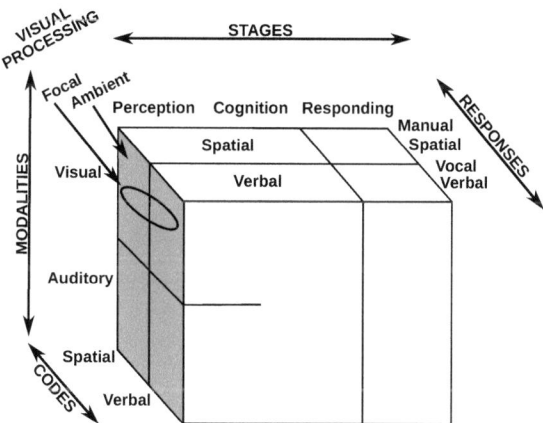

Figure 1: Cognitive Load Model (adapted from Wickens 2002: 163)

The result of this adaptation is a Cognitive Resource Footprint (CRF), which Seeber (2007) also develops for shadowing and sight-translation. Simultaneous interpreting is the combination of two main tasks: the listening and comprehension task on the one hand, and the production and monitoring task on the other. As

---

[7]Perception and cognition are considered as one dimension, as one cannot take place without the other.

shown in Figure 2, the first task mobilizes auditory-verbal and cognitive-verbal resources at the perceptual-cognitive stage (interpreters receive the aural stimulus, i.e. the words pronounced by the speaker, and analyze the verbal message). The second task requires the same kind of resources at the perceptual-cognitive stage and additional vocal-verbal resources at the response stage (interpreters verbally "respond" to what they have heard by delivering the message in the target language, but also listen to and monitor their own rendition).

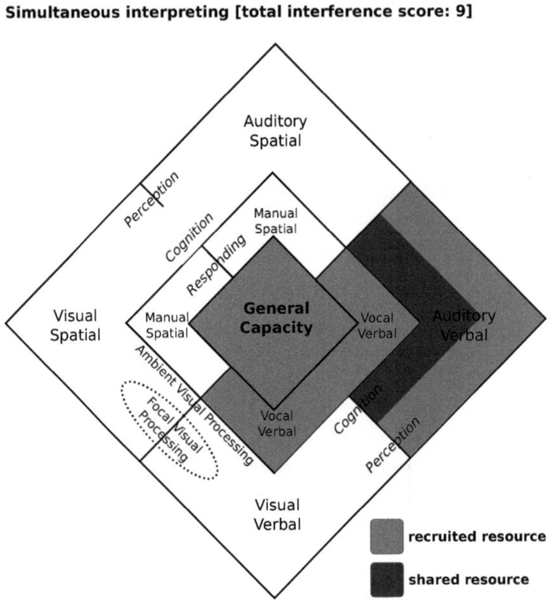

Figure 2: Cognitive resource footprint for simultaneous interpreting (adapted from Seeber 2007: 1385)

The footprint is integrated by a Conflict Matrix which shows the degree of interference between two co-occurring tasks as the sum of the demand vectors for each sub-task and of the individual conflict coefficients between sub-tasks (see Figure 3).

The demand vectors indicate the degree to which each sub-task recruits a certain type of resource. Seeber postulates a demand vector of 1 for each sub-task. Conflict coefficients instead show to which degree the single sub-tasks compete for the same resources. When two sub-tasks share resources that are governed by the same structures, their level of conflict is higher than for two sub-tasks that do not share resources (and time-sharing between them is not as efficient). The sum of demand vectors and conflict coefficients produces a value of 9 for simultaneous interpreting.

3 An exploratory study on CAI tools in simultaneous interpreting

				listening & comprehension							
				perceptual				cognitive		response	
		vector		∅	∅	∅	1	∅	1	∅	∅
	demand			visual spatial	visual verbal	auditory spatial	auditory verbal	cognitive spatial	cognitive verbal	response spatial	response verbal
perceptual		∅	visual spatial	0.8	0.6	0.6	0.4	0.7	0.5	0.4	0.2
		∅	visual verbal	0.6	0.8	0.4	0.6	0.5	0.7	0.2	0.4
		∅	auditory spatial	0.6	0.4	0.8	0.4	0.7	0.5	0.4	0.2
		1	auditory verbal	0.4	0.6	0.4	0.8	0.5	0.7	0.2	0.4
cognitive		∅	cognitive spatial	0.7	0.5	0.7	0.5	0.8	0.6	0.6	0.4
		1	cognitive verbal	0.5	0.7	0.5	0.7	0.6	0.8	0.4	0.6
response		∅	response spatial	0.4	0.2	0.4	0.2	0.6	0.4	0.8	0.6
		1	response verbal	0.2	0.4	0.2	0.4	0.4	0.6	0.6	1.0

Total interference score = demand vectors + conflict coefficients
= (1 + 1 + 1 + 1 + 1) + (0.7 + 0.8 + 0.4 + 0.6 + 0.8 + 0.7)

Figure 3: Conflict matrix for simultaneous interpreting (adapted from Seeber 2011: 188)

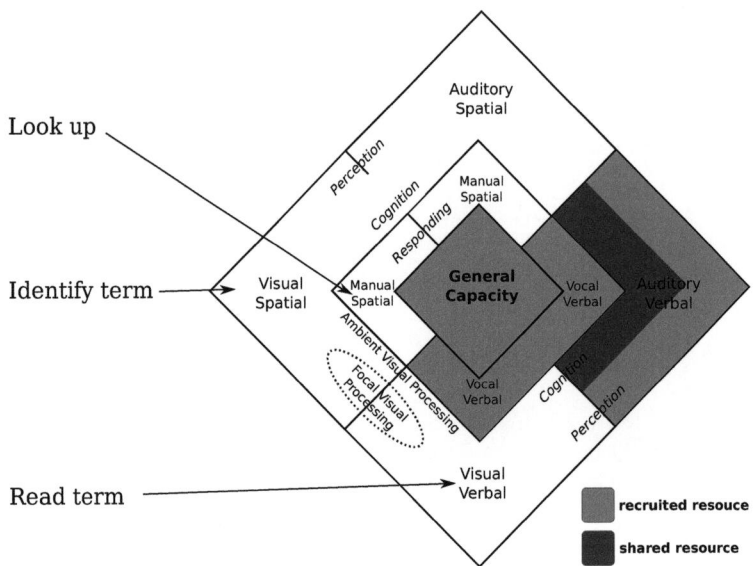

Figure 4: Additional cognitive resources recruited during SI with a CAI tool/electronic glossary

The possibility to "quantify" the degree of interference between co-occurring tasks and to explain multi-tasking makes Seeber's Cognitive Load Model more suited than Gile's EM to formulate hypotheses on simultaneous interpreting with CAI tools, as discussed below. For this reason, I chose the Cognitive Load Model for simultaneous interpreting as my theoretical framework.

2.2 Hypotheses on SI with CAI

Seeber uses his model to represent the allocation of cognitive resources during "standard" simultaneous interpreting, without indicating any specific conditions under which this activity is performed. What happens when, during SI, the interpreter can query a terminological database? What kind of cognitive resources are recruited, and at which stage? And how much do they interfere with each other?

In addition to the operations traditionally performed during simultaneous interpreting, when working with a CAI tool, or with another terminology management solution – such as an electronic glossary – the interpreter has to type a term or part thereof in order to query the database. This action can be considered as a response to the auditory stimulus, a reaction that precedes the vocal-verbal response (i.e. the interpreter's delivery of the term in question). During the look-up process, manual-spatial resources are therefore recruited at the response stage.

3 An exploratory study on CAI tools in simultaneous interpreting

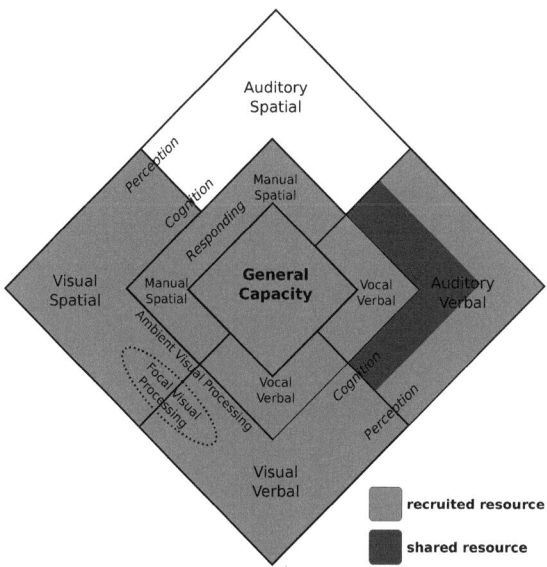

Figure 5: Cognitive Resource Footprint for SI with a CAI tool/electronic glossary

After the query has been completed, interpreters are typically presented with a list of terminological pairs (the term and its equivalent(s) in the target language). They will therefore need to visually identify on the screen the term needed, an operation that requires visual-spatial resources at the perceptive-cognitive stage. Once the term has been identified, it is also read, making use of visual-verbal resources in the same stage of the process. As illustrated by Figures 4 and 5, the Cognitive Resource Footprint for simultaneous interpreting during which a terminological query is performed using a CAI tool or an electronic glossary recruits more resources than "standard" SI.

It goes without saying that the CRF shown in Figure 5 applies only to those moments when the interpreter is performing a query, and should not be seen as representative of the whole interpreting process. Cognitive load is not static, but rather varies constantly during the interpreting process, as a function of the cognitive resources recruited. I hypothesize that cognitive load is higher while the query is performed, since more cognitive resources are recruited (as shown by the CRF). In some cases, it might even lead to cognitive overload. If the term retrieval is successful, however, I expect cognitive load to go back to normal levels during production. Cognitive load might even be lower than for "standard" simultaneous interpreting, as the search for the appropriate term in the interpreter's memory would be replaced by a query in the glossary.

production & monitoring		demand		listening & comprehension: perceptual				cognitive		response	
			vector	Ø	Ø	Ø	1	Ø	1	Ø	Ø
				visual spatial	visual verbal	auditory spatial	auditory verbal	cognitive spatial	cognitive verbal	response spatial	response verbal
perceptual	visual spatial	2		0.8	0.6	0.6	0.4	0.7	0.5	0.4	0.2
perceptual	visual verbal	2		0.6	0.8	0.4	0.6	0.5	0.7	0.2	0.4
perceptual	auditory spatial	Ø		0.6	0.4	0.8	0.4	0.7	0.5	0.4	0.2
perceptual	auditory verbal	1		0.4	0.6	0.4	0.8	0.5	0.7	0.2	0.4
cognitive	cognitive spatial	Ø		0.7	0.5	0.7	0.5	0.8	0.6	0.6	0.4
cognitive	cognitive verbal	1		0.5	0.7	0.5	0.7	0.6	0.8	0.4	0.6
response	response spatial	2		0.4	0.2	0.4	0.2	0.6	0.4	0.8	0.6
response	response verbal	1		0.2	0.4	0.2	0.4	0.4	0.6	0.6	1.0

Figure 6: Conflict matrix for SI with spreadsheet (Excel) TIC = 16.8

3 An exploratory study on CAI tools in simultaneous interpreting

			listening & comprehension							
			perceptual				cognitive		response	
		vector	∅	∅	∅	1	∅	1	∅	∅
	demand		visual spatial	visual verbal	auditory spatial	auditory verbal	cognitive spatial	cognitive verbal	response spatial	response verbal
perceptual	2	visual spatial	0.8	0.6	0.6	0.4	0.7	0.5	0.4	0.2
	2	visual verbal	0.6	0.8	0.4	0.6	0.5	0.7	0.2	0.4
	∅	auditory spatial	0.6	0.4	0.8	0.4	0.7	0.5	0.4	0.2
	1	auditory verbal	0.4	0.6	0.4	0.8	0.5	0.7	0.2	0.4
cognitive	∅	cognitive spatial	0.7	0.5	0.7	0.5	0.8	0.6	0.6	0.4
	1	cognitive verbal	0.5	0.7	0.5	0.7	0.6	0.8	0.4	0.6
response	2	response spatial	0.4	0.2	0.4	0.2	0.6	0.4	0.8	0.6
	1	response verbal	0.2	0.4	0.2	0.4	0.4	0.6	0.6	1.0

Figure 7: Conflict matrix for SI with CAI (InterpretBank) TIC = 14.8

If one only took into consideration the Cognitive Resource Footprint, one would not, however, be able to formulate hypotheses on the differences in Cognitive Load experienced while working with a CAI tool or with less advanced terminology management solutions, such as electronic glossaries in the form of a Word or Excel table. These differences can be explored by assigning a different demand vector to the various terminology management solutions. The Conflict Matrices can thus help visually represent the different levels of recruitment of cognitive resources. If the glossary is the same, what varies among the tools are the user interface and the search algorithm. The most advanced CAI tools, and InterpretBank[8] in particular, which I adopt in the study, are designed to yield the most accurate results and to facilitate the user in identifying the term needed on the screen. I therefore expect the tools to require a lower level of manual-spatial resources (to look up the term) and of visual-spatial resources (to locate the term on the screen), when compared, for instance, to an Excel spreadsheet. As shown in Figures 6 and 7, I can therefore assign a demand vector of 1 to each of these resources in the case of CAI tools, and a demand vector of 2 in the case of an Excel spreadsheet. The total interference score for SI performed during the use of a CAI tool would therefore be equal to 14.8, while for SI with the use of an Excel spreadsheet it would be higher (16.8).

The integration of automatic speech recognition in a CAI tool (see Fantinuoli 2017b) would require no manual-spatial resources, thus lowering the total interference score to at least 13.2.

3 Designing a pilot study on the use of CAI tools in the booth

3.1 Introduction

The debate around how CAI tools influence the process and the quality of interpretation is in large measure not based on empirical data, which are still very scarce and limited to a few small experiments, but is rather the result of personal beliefs and assumptions which have not been proven empirically. A research project currently underway at the University of Mainz/Germersheim (Prandi 2016; 2017b,a) aims at bridging this research gap by providing data that can substantiate arguments in favor and against CAI tools. One source of difficulty in the investigation of CAI tools lies in the fact that no research methodology for the combined collection of data both on the process and on the product of SI with CAI has been devel-

---

[8]http://www.interpretbank.com

oped and tested yet. In order to provide a first solution to this issue, I therefore conducted an exploratory study with the aim of evaluating the appropriateness of the stimuli used for data collection. In the following sections I will present my research questions, describe the structure of the exploratory study and illustrate the stimuli used. The analysis of the participants' renditions is the subject of the remainder of the chapter.

3.2 Research questions

My research project aims at answering three fundamental questions:

- Do CAI tools help improve the terminological quality of the interpretation when compared to traditional electronic glossaries?

- Does a query performed with a CAI tool during SI lead to lower additional local cognitive load when compared to traditional glossary prepared with Word or Excel? Does looking up terminology lead to cognitive overload and if so, does this also happen when CAI tools are used?

- Can a combination of eye-tracking measures, key-logging data and transcription analysis be used to acquire data on the interpreting process, the terminological quality of the product and the usability of CAI tools?

In order to first collect data to help answer these questions, an exploratory study was conducted between May and July 2017 at the University of Mainz/Germersheim. For the scope of this paper, I will report on the observations made during the analysis of the product, while further work will be required to address the issues related to the process of simultaneous interpreting with CAI tools.

3.3 Structure of the study: sample, duration, training and data collection

The pilot study involved 6 advanced students of the Master's degree in conference interpreting of the University of Mainz/Germersheim. Prior to the study, all students had had at least 3 semesters of practice in simultaneous and consecutive interpreting and had English in their combination as a B or C language. Half of the sample was made up of German natives (one male and two females), half of Italian natives (one female and two males). The test subjects were recruited by e-mail and their participation in the experiment was voluntary. No monetary compensation was offered, but the participation in the study gave the trainees the opportunity to learn about a new tool, InterpretBank, and to practice in the booth with a laptop, something they rarely do systematically in class.

The trainees attended one preliminary meeting which covered the basics of terminology management for conference interpreters. The presentation was centered on practice rather than theory, since a previous study confirmed this was more beneficial to achieve a good level of expertise (Prandi 2015a,b). The search functions in Word, Excel and InterpretBank were described in detail. For the purpose of the study, participants could visualize all the results of a query when working with Word[9], while they had to move to the next occurrence when using Excel. In the presentation I made sure to adopt a neutral approach to the different tools, so as not to favor the CAI tool chosen.

After covering the basics, 5 practice sessions followed in the subsequent weeks, with around 1 session per week. During each training session, the students interpreted 3 short speeches from English into their mother tongue (either German or Italian). They could use a glossary provided by the author, for both language combinations, which they could access in all three formats (Word, Excel or InterpretBank). During each session, they used a different tool for each speech, so equal practice time was dedicated to each tool. The first few speeches had been prepared ad-hoc by the author for a previous study (Prandi 2015a,b), while the last few speeches were authentic speeches selected by the author, so as to ensure a certain progression in the practice material. The topics covered during the practice sessions were medicine and biology. After the last session, the students took a short test to verify their proficiency in the use of the tools. All students passed the test and were deemed ready for data collection.

Data collection took place in the *Translation and Cognition Centre* of the University of Mainz/Germersheim. The test subjects were briefed about the structure of the study and were informed that they were going to interpret 3 speeches from English into their mother tongue. They were told the topic of the speeches (renewables and other sources of energy) right before data collection started. While this does not reflect professional practice, which requires thorough preparation before interpretation proper, the students were not given the chance to prepare in advance since this would have introduced an additional variable in the study. The methods of preparation and the time dedicated to this fundamental phase of interpreting are very personal and would have been very difficult to standardize and to verify. I therefore decided to sacrifice some ecological validity to limit the number of independent variables.

Every test subject interpreted 3 speeches, each about 12 minutes long and with an average speed of 122.26 words per minute. This speed was chosen to make sure

---

[9] The results are displayed in a column on the left-hand side of the window.

that looking up terminology during interpreting was challenging, but not impossible. All three speeches had been prepared ad-hoc for the study and previously recorded by a native speaker of British English. One glossary of 421 terms was prepared by the author. It contained the same terms for both language combinations and had a simple tabular structure – one column for the source language and one for the target language. The glossary was prepared with InterpretBank and then exported as an Excel spreadsheet, which was then also converted into a Word table. The glossaries were not shown to the test subjects before the interpreting task started. During the interpreting task, the screen was divided in two areas. On the left-hand side, the test subjects could see the video of the speaker, which served as a fixation cross when no term query was being performed. The glossary window was placed on the right-hand side of the screen.

The test subjects' deliveries were recorded with Audacity, while an SMI RED250M eye-tracker was used to record eye movements. A LOG file, automatically created by InterpretBank, served as a reference to check what terms had been looked up by the test subjects. The same was done manually for the trials in which Word and Excel were adopted, using the Gaze Replay recordings. The interpretations were then transcribed using Partitur Editor, the transcription tool of the Exmaralda suite, and then analyzed. Before presenting the method used for this analysis and its results in §5, I will describe the main features of the speeches used for data collection, with a focus on stimuli distribution and morphological complexity.

4 Stimuli features and distribution

While asking the test subjects to interpret single terms would have eliminated the time constraint typical of simultaneous interpreting, working with authentic, unedited speeches would have introduced too many variables in the experiment. For this reason, I decided to adapt Seeber's methodology (2011) by creating ad-hoc speeches made up of sentence clusters. This method presents three main advantages. First, it enables me to focus the investigation on the target sentences (i.e. the ones which include the stimulus). Second, it makes it easier to work with comparable speeches, as they have the same structure. Third, it gives the test subjects the impression that they are interpreting a speech, rather than disconnected sentences, thus helping me retain a certain degree of ecological validity. Each sentence cluster is composed of a general, introductory sentence, followed by the target sentence containing the stimulus, followed by a third sentence which, like the first one, does not contain specialized terminology. The structure is repeated throughout the speech, so that each stimulus is separated from the next one by two sentences. Here is an example from speech no. 1:

(1) So we need to change this basic trend and this is why the urgency is there.
In our policies, we should definitely address the need to improve **vehicle efficiency**.
But there is still much more we can do, in many other areas, as you are aware.
At the EU level, there is another policy option that can help us.
By focusing, for instance, on **woody biomass fuels**, we can truly make a difference.
They have the potential to help us respond to the challenges we're facing.

Each speech prepared for data collection contained 36 terms, 12 of which are unigrams (e.g. "bioenergy"), 12 bigrams (e.g. "energy poverty") and 12 trigrams (e.g. "pressurized water reactor"). This variable was introduced because the structure of the stimuli is expected to also play a role in the usability of the tools. I expect there to be differences between tools when a more morphologically complex term is looked up – it should be more difficult to find a trigram when using a Word or an Excel glossary than when working with a CAI tool.

Of each group of stimuli, 6 are placed at the end of the sentence and 6 in the middle of the sentence. This was done to verify whether the stimulus position has an impact on cognitive load and on the test subjects' behavior in querying the glossary. I expect the stimuli placed at the end of the sentence to lead to a lower increase in cognitive load and to be looked up more often, thanks to anticipation.

Of the 6 terms placed at the end of the sentence, 3 should require a query in the glossary, because they are less frequent and thus probably unknown to the participants, and 3 should not.[10] The same is true for the terms placed in the middle of the sentence. Half of the stimuli in each speech should therefore require a query and half should not. This variable was introduced to verify whether CAI tools, which are usually deemed to be user-friendlier and to take up fewer cognitive resources, allow participants to perform more queries without leading to a higher number of errors or omissions. Figure 8 sums up the features of the stimuli and their distribution in each speech. For each speech, the stimuli can thus be classified according to their features, for future analysis. Table 1 shows an example of this classification for the stimuli in speech nr. 1.

---

[10] This classification was based on the frequency of the terms as per the 2015 news corpus, the 2012 web corpus (UK) and the 2016 Wikipedia corpus for the English language (Projekt Deutscher Wortschatz, http://wortschatz.uni-leipzig.de).

3 An exploratory study on CAI tools in simultaneous interpreting

Table 1: Stimuli classification – speech 1

Stimulus	Position	Morphological complexity	Glossary search needed (GS)
bioenergy	E	1	
security of supply	M	3	
gasoline	M	1	
conventional fossil fuels	M	3	
vehicle efficiency	E	2	X
woody biomass fuels	M	3	X
liquid biofuels	E	2	
rapeseed methyl ester	E	3	X
transesterification	E	1	X
short-rotation coppice	E	3	X
black liquor	E	2	X
corn stover	E	2	X
lignocellulosic solid biomass	E	3	X
gasification	M	1	X
gasifier	E	1	
green charcoal	M	2	X
briquettes	M	1	X
biofuels sector	M	2	
soil protection	E	2	
petroleum	M	1	
greenhouse gas emissions	E	3	
EU biofuels directive	M	3	X
indicative targets	M	2	X
incentives	E	1	
set-aside land	M	3	X
arable land	M	2	
solar power	M	2	
second-generation biofuels	E	3	
switchgrass	E	1	X
first-generation biofuels	E	3	
residue cake	M	2	X
milling	E	1	X
malting	M	1	X
overall energy demand	M	3	
renewables	M	1	
energy mix	E	2	

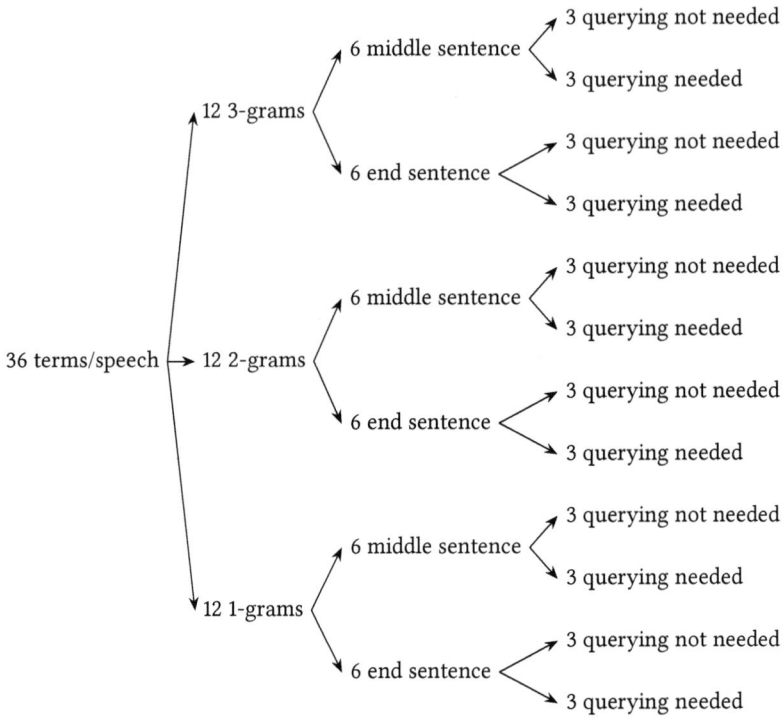

Figure 8: Features and distribution of the stimuli used for data collection

5 Stimuli validation

One of the aims of the exploratory study was to verify whether the stimuli prepared for data collection, to be also used in a future experiment involving a larger sample, elicited the reaction I expected from the test subjects, i.e. a query in the glossary. This is necessary to make sure that enough queries are performed in the glossary to provide sufficient data for a comparison between the three terminology management solutions I focus my analysis on – Word glossaries, Excel glossaries and second-generation CAI tools. While a certain degree of inter-subject variability can be expected, I must verify whether my a-priori classification of the stimuli holds true on a general level. This is the focus of the first part of the transcription analysis which will be presented in §5.1.

Another goal of my research is to verify whether the use of a CAI tool leads to better terminological quality in comparison to more traditional terminology management solutions, e.g. Word and Excel glossaries. First observations made in the sample are briefly discussed in §5.2, where I also provide a framework to analyze errors and omissions in relation to the tools used for glossary query.

§5.3 presents the results of my observations in relation to the strategies adopted by the test subjects to interpret the stimuli. Given the small size of the sample, with this exploratory study I aim to develop a methodology to be used for further research, rather than to draw conclusions, which will require a larger data set.

5.1 Stimuli classification

As previously stated, half of the stimuli were classified as needing a glossary query. In order to verify whether this was true, the sample was checked for the total number of terms searched, the number of terms searched that were classified as needing to be searched in the glossary ("QN") and the number of terms searched that I did not expect to require a query in the glossary ("NO QN").

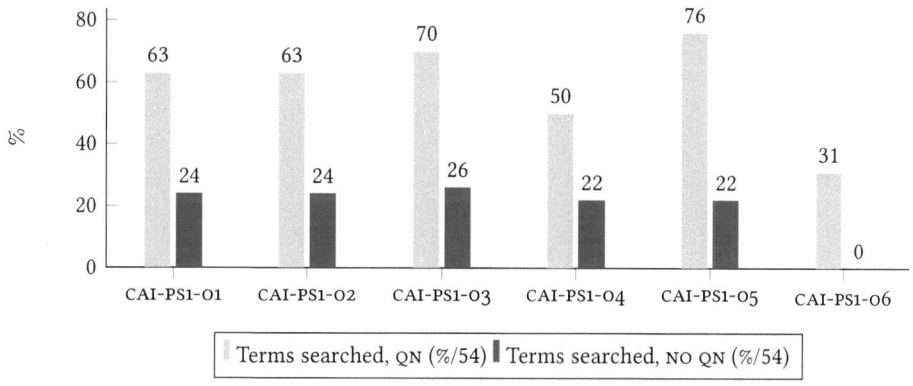

Figure 9: Search behavior per stimuli category

As shown in Figure 9, the percentage of terms classified as needing a query that were actually searched varies among the test subjects, while it is quite similar in the case of terms classified as not needing a query. A notable exception is test subject CAI-PS1-06, who searched a much lower number of terms than the other test subjects. The percentages are very similar for the German natives (participants CAI-PS1-01, CAI-PS1-02 and CAI-PS1-03), although they looked up different terms.

I also verified which terms classified as needing a glossary query had not been looked up by any subject. 5 terms out of 54 were not looked up by anyone and should therefore either be moved to the non-query category or replaced by more specialized, less frequent terms. Of the terms classified as not needing a query in the glossary, only 1 out of 54 was looked up by all test subjects. It should therefore either be classified differently or replaced.

If we take into consideration the position of the stimuli in the target sentences, something interesting emerges from this data analysis, which deserves further exploration in a bigger sample, especially in correlation with eye-tracking data. While the difference is more evident for some test subjects than for others, the stimuli placed at the end of the sentence seem to elicit more queries than the stimuli placed in the middle of the sentence (see Figure 10). This might be explained with the fact that, when a term is placed at the end of the sentence, anticipation might lead the participants to prepare themselves to adopt a coping mechanism, such as a glossary query. The "preparation" could also result in a sentence structure that favors a glossary query, requiring less restructuring or making it difficult to omit the term completely. This could, however, result in higher cognitive load, because if the query is not successful, more cognitive resources would be needed to adopt a different strategy, possibly affecting the rendition of the following sentences. A stimulus placed in the middle of the sentence could prompt the interpreter to immediately choose a strategy different than consulting the glossary available, such as generalization or the use of a synonym. While this may lead to a less precise rendition of the original, it may also come with lower cognitive load experienced.

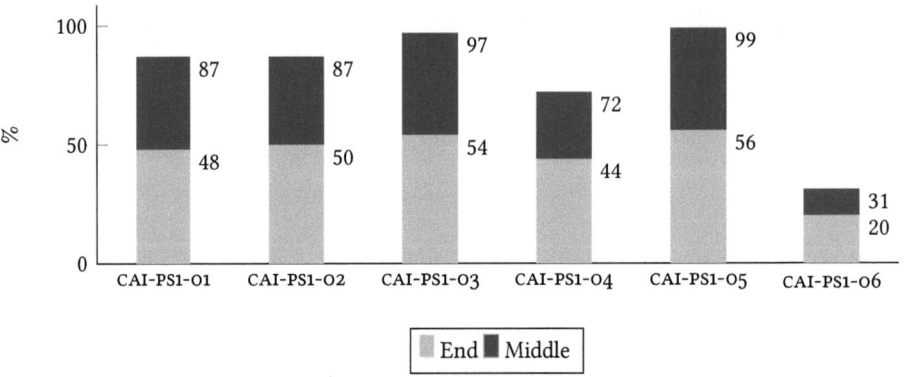

Figure 10: Stimulus position and percentage of terms searched. Percentage expressed on a total of 54 terms per category.

Even though the stimuli classified as requiring a query were equally distributed in terms of position – half of them placed in the middle and half at the end of the sentence – the difference in the search behavior might also be due to the terms themselves, rather than only to their position. This can be further tested

3 An exploratory study on CAI tools in simultaneous interpreting

on a larger sample by switching the position of the stimuli or by using a different set of stimuli.

If we take into consideration the morphological complexity – here defined as the number of elements making up the terms[11] – we notice that unigrams are searched more often than bigrams and trigrams in the case of the stimuli classified as not needing a query (see Figure 11). This might be explained with the fact that, when faced with a bigram or a trigram, participants need to decide which element of the term should be looked up, which requires additional cognitive resources. For this reason, they might choose to directly adopt a different strategy. A unigram does not require them to make this decision, and so the act of querying the glossary is more straightforward. No clear trend can be identified for the stimuli that should require a query.

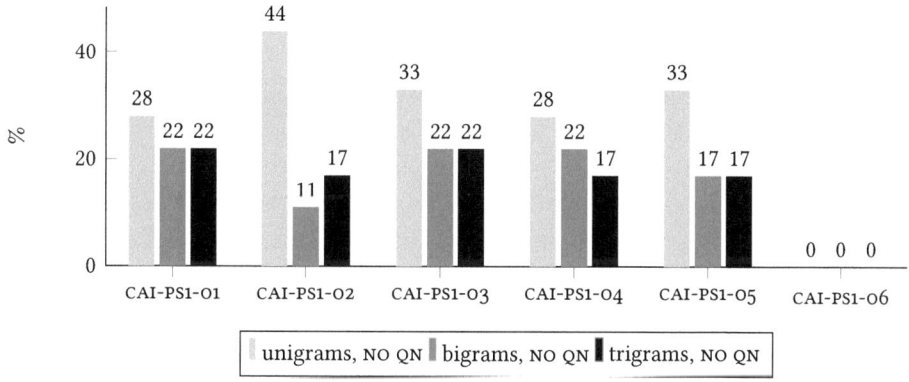

Figure 11: Morphological complexity and percentage of terms searched (terms not needing a query). N=18/category

All in all, my a-priori classification of the stimuli was confirmed by the sample, if I exclude the outlier CAI-PS1-06. Further research will be needed to check the hypotheses on the role played by the position and the morphological complexity of the stimuli.

5.2 Tools used and precision of renditions

With the aim of gaining initial data on how the tool used influences the precision of the test subjects' renditions, I compared the level of precision observed for the Word glossary, the Excel glossary and InterpretBank, when a glossary query was chosen as the strategy to interpret the terms. My classification of the renditions is loosely based on Wadensjö (1998) and is made up of 3 main categories:

---

[11]For instance, a trigram is considered morphologically more complex than a bigram.

Close renditions (precision 2 – P2): no information lost, precise rendition, use of equivalent as per glossary or adequate synonym

Acceptable renditions (precision 1 – P1): some information is lost (e.g. through paraphrasing, the loss of an adjective in trigrams, a drop in register), but the general meaning is maintained

Zero/unacceptable rendition (precision 0 – P0): the rendition completely or largely deviates from the original message (the content is different), or the information is not present (zero rendition).

This classification certainly presents some degree of subjectivity, but it is nonetheless useful as a broad guideline to evaluate the precision of the test subjects' deliveries. Figures 12, 13 and 14 sum up the degree of terminological precision achieved when performing a glossary query with Word, Excel and InterpretBank glossaries.

Inter-subject variability is too high to draw initial conclusions on this aspect, but Excel seems to lead to the worst performance, since one can notice more occurrences of zero renditions or unacceptable renditions than for Word and InterpretBank. This is probably due to the fact that, when working with Excel, test subjects did not have the possibility to view all the results of a query, but only to manually skip to the next occurrence, which might make the query too cumbersome to be performed in the very short amount of time available to the interpreter. InterpretBank seems to perform slightly better than Word, but this should be further verified. Usability probably plays a role in this respect, so eye-tracking measures will be key in determining how the user interface facilitates or hinders the identification of the equivalent needed.

As for the morphological complexity, I expected queries performed with InterpretBank to be more effective – leading to a higher level of precision – than queries performed with Word and Excel, especially for more complex terms (trigrams). In the small sample analyzed in the pilot study, queries performed with InterpretBank lead to higher precision for unigrams in 5 out of 6 cases. The only exception is participant CAI-PS1-06, for whom there are very few data points when compared to the rest of the sample. For bigrams and trigrams the results are less uniform – queries with InterpretBank are more effective than Word and Excel in 3 participants out of 6. While the sample analyzed is too small to draw conclusions, this aspect can be further analyzed in a larger sample, where differences might be significant.

It should be noted that in order to facilitate the analysis, I first took into consideration only the terms and the content conveyed by them, not by the whole

3 An exploratory study on CAI tools in simultaneous interpreting

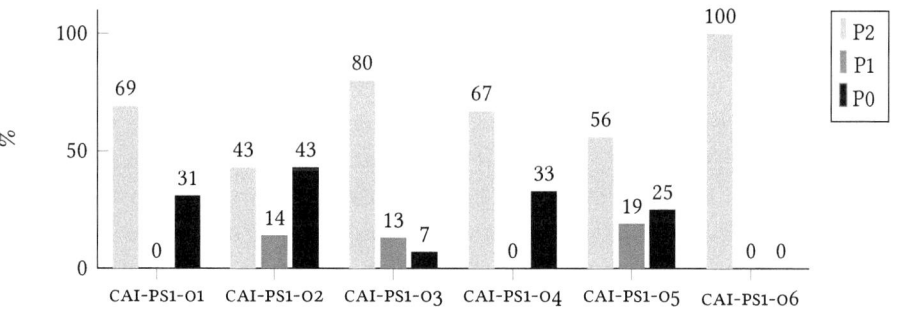

Figure 12: Precision of renditions with Word

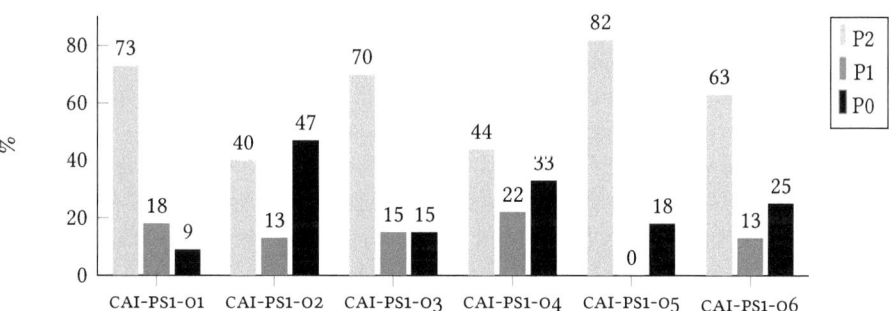

Figure 13: Precision of renditions with Excel

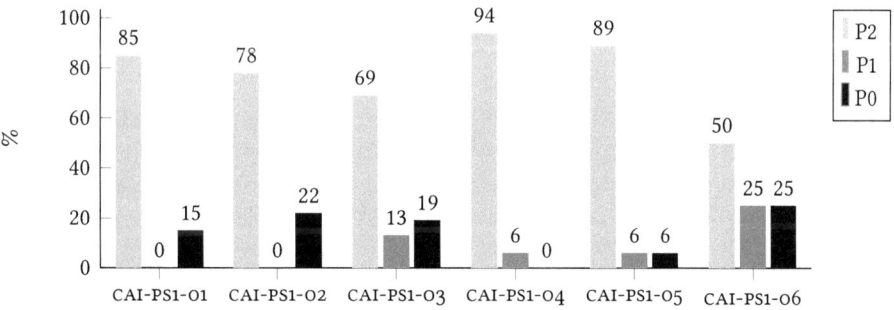

Figure 14: Precision of renditions with InterpretBank

sentences. This analysis hence remains focused at a microscopic level, that of terminology. Since the ultimate goal of CAI tools is that of improving the overall quality of the rendition, I deem it necessary to expand my analysis to the sentence level, to verify whether a higher level of precision achieved in the rendition of the terminological unit results in a correct and complete rendition of the sentence it is embedded in – and of the following ones – or whether, on the contrary, the query, despite being successful, leads to errors or omissions. To this aim, the transcriptions of the test subjects' renditions were annotated following Barik's (1971) classification of omissions, additions and errors in SI. In the data analysis, I decided to focus on three categories which represent the most serious issues encountered in the rendition, namely E4 (substantial phrasing change), E5 (gross phrasing change) and a third category which corresponds to a complete omission of the sentence, which I labeled as M5.[12] On the other hand, to make the analysis easier, I grouped in one category the renditions that did not present any issue or only presented less serious issues, such as skipping omissions and mild phrasing changes. The classification of errors and omissions provides an element of subjectivity which might be constrained by taking into consideration only clearly wrong sentences or total omissions.

Given the small sample of the study and the subsequent high level of inter-subject variability in the number of terms searched, I was not able to identify any clear trends from this data alone. The statistical significance of the data will have to be verified on a bigger sample. Nonetheless, the pilot study was useful to define a working method that can be applied to further research and possibly expanded to also take into consideration the features of the stimuli.

5.3 Tools used and interpreting strategies

I conclude my analysis by looking at the strategies adopted, to establish whether a correlation can be found with the tools used. The classification of the interpreting strategies is based on Bartłomiejczyk (2006). In my analysis, I focused on the "strategies of production" (ibid.), which can be observed by analyzing the product of SI, while I did not take into consideration overall strategies, which would require additional methods to be identified. From the analysis of the transcriptions, 10 main strategies, or coping-tactics (Gile 1995), emerged:

1. Glossary search (GS)

2. Approximation (A): use of a synonym or a closely related term

---

[12] See Barik (1971) for a complete classification of errors, omissions and additions in SI.

3. Compression (C): use of a hyperonym, some precision is missing

4. Omission (O): not strictly considered a strategy, it is mostly unintentional

5. Paraphrase (P)

6. Reproduction (R): no translation, the term is reported as in the source language

7. Transfer (T): ad-hoc translation

8. Syntactic transformation (ST)

9. World knowledge (WK): reference to one's pre-existing knowledge

10. Substitution (S): the term is replaced by another term, not related to it

Figure 15 reports an overview of the strategies used by the test subjects for all tools and all stimuli. The data clearly shows that, with one exception, a glossary query was the strategy most used by the test subjects. This can be easily explained by the fact that the test subjects had not prepared for the assignment. The second most used strategies are approximation, omission and world knowledge.

The third most used strategies are world knowledge, paraphrase and omission.

Looking at the strategies adopted when using different tools to look up terms in the glossary, one can notice that, when using InterpretBank (see Figure 18), a glossary query is the favorite strategy, except for one subject (the same as in the general analysis), who seems to resort mainly to approximation. The second most used strategies are omission and approximation, while the third most used strategies are world knowledge and approximation.

Querying the glossary was the favorite strategy also when Excel (Figure 17) was used, in 4 cases out of 6, while the other two resorted, respectively, mainly to omission and paraphrase, and to world knowledge. There is not a clear preference as to the second most used strategy, but omission and paraphrasing prevail, while the third most used, in 4 cases out of 6, is world knowledge, followed by approximation and both omission and compression.

In the third case, in which the test subjects could look up terms in a Word glossary (see Figure 16), a glossary query also seems to be the favorite strategy, while paraphrasing, omission and world knowledge are the second most used strategies in the sample. The third most used strategy strategies are omission and compression.

Bianca Prandi

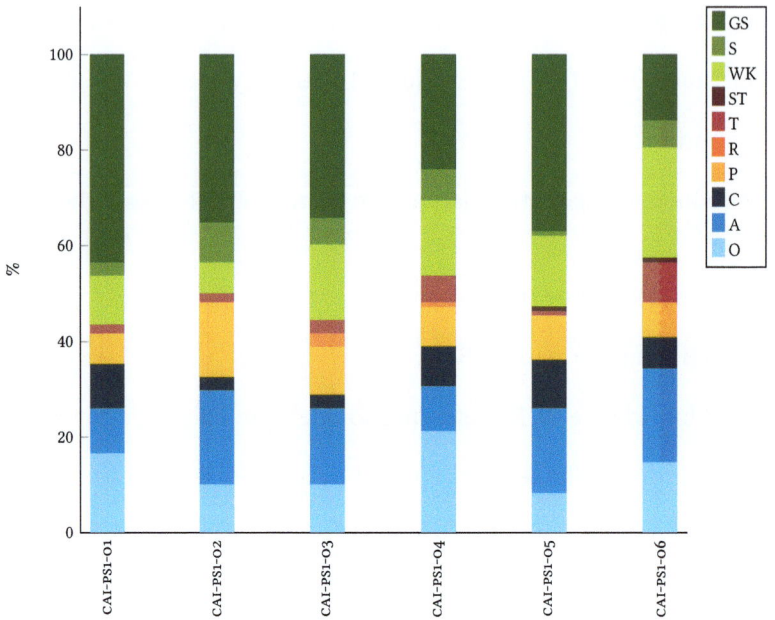

Figure 15: Overview of strategies used (all tools and stimuli)

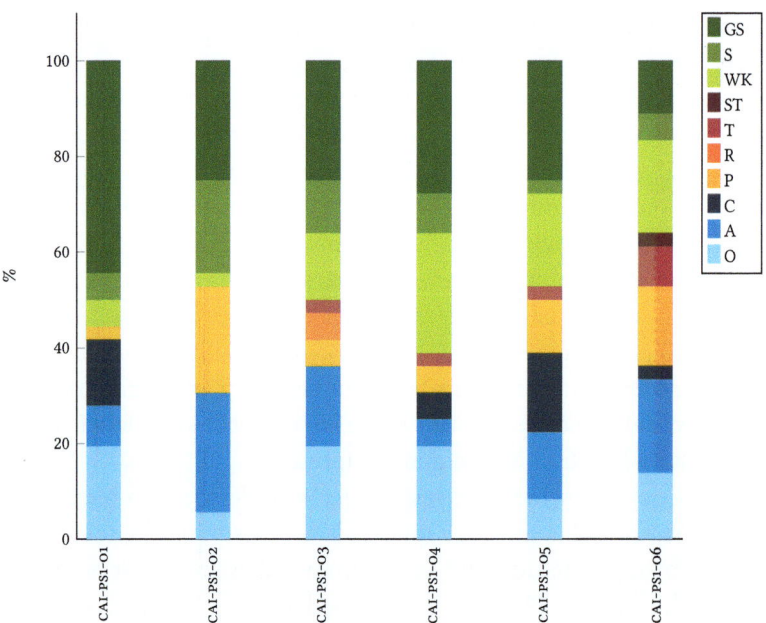

Figure 16: Strategies adopted – Word glossary

3 An exploratory study on CAI tools in simultaneous interpreting

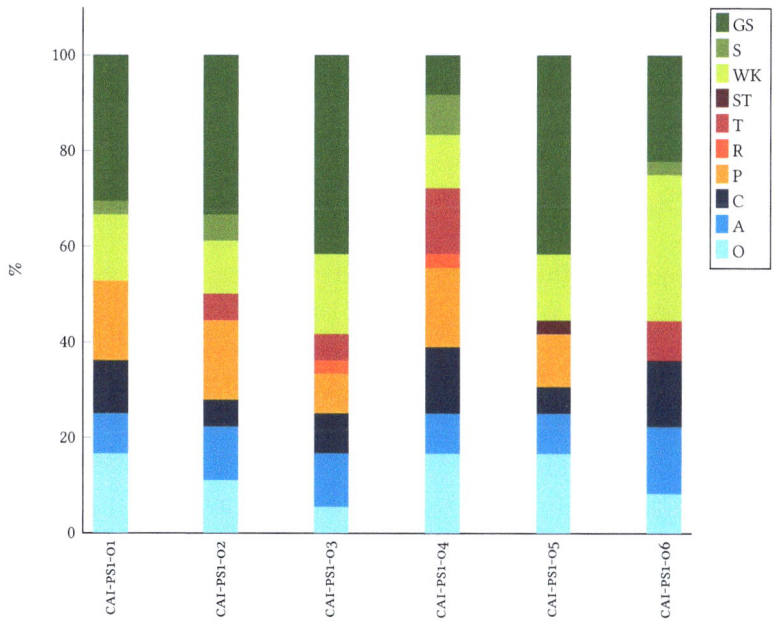

Figure 17: Strategies adopted – Excel glossary

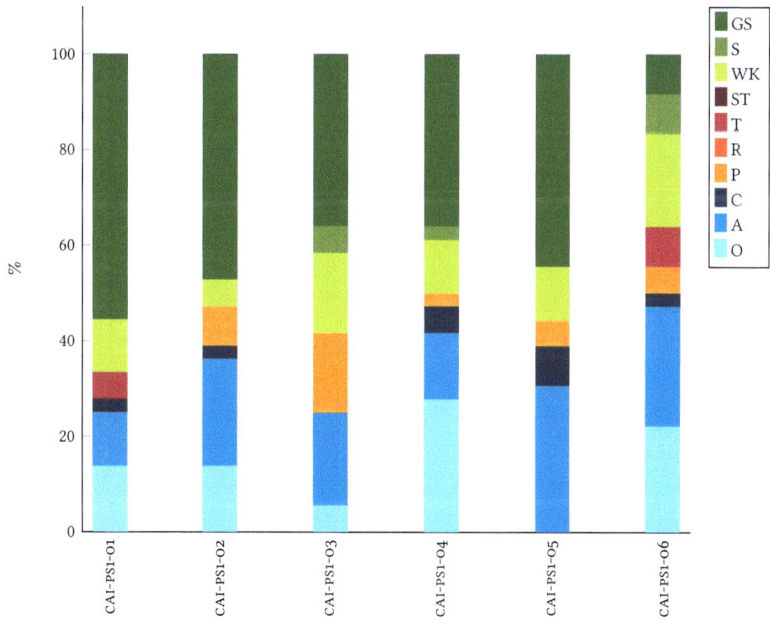

Figure 18: Strategies adopted – InterpretBank glossary

Even though a glossary search was the preferred strategy by almost all participants irrespective of the tool used, the percentage of queries performed with InterpretBank seems to be higher across the board, except for one participant. By looking at these initial data, I can thus hypothesize that test subjects find it easier to perform a glossary query when using InterpretBank, probably due to better usability, and that reference to previous knowledge, approximation, paraphrasing, compression or outright omission are the preferred coping tactics when the glossary is not queried. This should be tested on a larger sample by triangulating data from transcriptions with eye-tracking data.

6 Conclusions and further research

The paper presented first results from an exploratory study aimed at developing a research methodology to investigate the use of computer-assisted interpreting tools during simultaneous interpreting. The pilot study is part of a PhD research project that aims at collecting data on both the procedural and the terminological aspect of SI with CAI, combining product- and process-based measures.

After discussing the theoretical framework chosen for the study, I presented my main hypotheses on cognitive load during SI with CAI. In particular, I expect cognitive load to be higher during SI with CAI than during traditional SI, but to be lower for CAI tools such as InterpretBank than for traditional terminology management solutions like Word and Excel glossaries. I also expect the terminological quality to be better when a CAI tool is used. While the hypotheses on cognitive load will require the analysis of eye-tracking data to be verified, the analysis of the interpretations helped shed some light on the terminological quality of SI performed with the support of CAI tools and of traditional table glossaries.

First data from the transcriptions of the test subjects' deliveries have proved helpful to verify the adequacy of the stimuli created for the experiment, showing that the a-priori classification of the stimuli used is overall confirmed by the test subjects' search behavior, in particular when it comes to the stimuli classification into terms expected to require a glossary query and terms not requiring a query. The position of the stimuli seems to play a role in the search behavior, while their morphological complexity does not seem to have a significant impact on it. InterpretBank seems to provide the highest degree of precision, and the glossary query appears to be the favorite kind of strategy to apply to cope with specialized terms when InterpretBank can be used to search for terminology. All of these aspects will need to be further investigated in future studies.

Further analysis of process-related and usability data, in particular of eye-tracking measures, will be necessary to gain information that can shed some light on the hypotheses on cognitive load and help formulate further hypotheses.

Finally, future studies should also include the option to query the glossary through automatic speech recognition which can be expected to be the most "cost-effective" option in terms of cognitive load added and level of precision, coherence and cohesion achieved in the interpretation.

References

Barik, Henri C. 1971. A description of various types of omissions, additions, and errors of translation encountered in simultaneous interpretation. *Meta* 16(4). 199–210.

Bartłomiejczyk, Magdalena. 2006. Strategies of simultaneous interpreting and directionality. *Interpreting* 2(8). 149–174.

Biagini, Giulio. 2015. *Glossario cartaceo e glossario elettronico durante l'interpretazione simultanea: Uno studio comparativo*. Università di Trieste MA thesis.

Costa, Hernani, Gloria Corpas Pastor & Isabel Durán-Muñoz. 2018. Assessing terminology management systems for interpreters. In Gloria Corpas Pastor & Isabel Durán-Muñoz (eds.), *Trends in E-tools and resources for translators and interpreters*, 57–84. Leiden: Brill.

De Merulis, Gianpiero. 2013. *L'uso di InterpretBank per la preparazione di una conferenza sul trattamento delle acque reflue: Gossario terminologico e contributo sperimentale*. Università di Bologna MA thesis.

Fantinuoli, Claudio. 2017a. Computer-assisted preparation in conference interpreting. *Translation & Interpreting* 9(2). 24–37.

Fantinuoli, Claudio. 2017b. Speech recognition in the interpreter workstation. In *Proceedings of the Translating and the Computer 39 Conference*, 367–377. London: Editions Tradulex.

Fantinuoli, Claudio. 2018. Computer-assisted interpreting: Challenges and future perspectives. In Gloria Corpas Pastor & Isabel Durán-Muñoz (eds.), *Trends in E-tools and resources for translators and interpreters*, 153–174. Leiden: Brill.

Gile, Daniel. 1988. Le partage de l'attention et le 'modèle d'effort' en interprétation simultanée. *The Interpreters' Newsletter* 1. 4–22.

Gile, Daniel. 1995. *Basic concepts and models for interpreter and translator training*. Amsterdam/Philadelphia: John Benjamins.

Gile, Daniel. 1997. Conference interpreting as a cognitive management problem. In Joseph H. Danks, Gregory M. Shreve, Stephen B. Fountain & Michael McBeath (eds.), *Cognitive processes in translation and interpretation*, 196–214. London: Sage.

Gile, Daniel. 1999. Testing the tight rope hypothesis in simultaneous interpreting – A contribution. *Hermes* 23. 153–172.

Kahneman, Daniel. 1973. *Attention and effort*. Englewood Cliffs, NJ: Prentice-Hall.

Kantowitz, Barry H. & J. L. Knight. 1976. Testing tapping timesharing: Auditory secondary task. *Acta Psychologica* 40(1). 343–362.

Prandi, Bianca. 2015a. *L'uso di InterpretBank nella didattica dell'interpretazione: Uno studio esplorativo*. Università di Bologna MA thesis.

Prandi, Bianca. 2015b. The use of CAI tools in interpreters' training: A pilot study. In *Proceedings of the Translating and the Computer 37 Conference*. Geneva: Editions Tradulex.

Prandi, Bianca. 2016. *Analysis of the impact of CAI tools on simultaneous interpreting with a focus on cognitive processes and terminology consistency*. Poster presented at TRA&CO Symposium, Johannes Gutenberg University. Mainz/Germersheim.

Prandi, Bianca. 2017a. Designing a multimethod study on the use of CAI tools during simultaneous interpreting. In *Proceedings of the Translating and the Computer 39 Conference*. Geneva: Editions Tradulex.

Prandi, Bianca. 2017b. *Investigating cognitive load in simultaneous interpreting with the support of terminology management tools*. Poster presented at 5th Polish Eye Tracking Conference Lublin. Lublin.

Rütten, Anja. 2007. *Informations- und Wissensmanagement im Konferenzdolmetschen*. Frankfurt am Main: Peter Lang.

Seeber, Kilian G. 2007. Thinking outside the cube: Modelling language processing tasks in a multiple resource paradigm. In *8th annual conference of the international speech communication association*, 1382–1385. Antwerp: Interspeech.

Seeber, Kilian G. 2011. Cognitive load in simultaneous interpreting: Existing theories – new models. *Interpreting* 13(2). 176–204.

Wadensjö, Cecilia. 1998. *Interpreting as interaction*. London: Longman.

Wickens, Christopher D. 1976. The effects of divided attention on information processing in tracking. *Journal of Experimental Psychology: Human Perception and Performance* 2. 1–13.

Wickens, Christopher D. 1984. Processing resources in attention. In Raja Parasuraman & David R. Davies (eds.), *Varieties of attention*, 63–102. New York: Academic Press.

Wickens, Christopher D. 2002. Multiple resources and performance prediction. *Theoretical issues in ergonomics science* 3(2). 159–177.

Will, Martin. 2009. *Dolmetschorientierte Terminologiearbeit: Modell und Methode.* Tübingen: Gunter Narr Verlag.

Will, Martin. 2015. Zur Eignung simultanfähiger Terminologiesysteme für das Konferenzdolmetschen. *Zeitschrift für Translationswissenschaft und Fachkommunikation* 8(1). 179–201.

Xu, Ran. 2018. Corpus-based terminological preparation for simultaneous interpreting. *Interpreting* 20(1). 29–58.

Chapter 4

Experimenting with computer-assisted interpreter training tools for the development of self-assessment skills: National Parliament of RSA

Elizabeth Deysel
National Parliament of South Africa

Harold Lesch
University of Stellenbosch

> This article explores the use of CAIT as a tool in the development of self-assessment skills in interpreting performance. The aim of this pilot study is to investigate and evaluate the effectiveness of the CAIT software in the development of self-assessment skills of practicing interpreters in the National Parliament of the Republic of South Africa. The results indicate that the practicing interpreters which were exposed to the software displayed an improvement in their self-assessment skills and they indicated a better understanding of the criteria which are important in the assessment of interpreting performance as well as a better awareness of the strengths and weaknesses in the interpreters' interpreting performance. The study concludes that CAIT may prove a viable tool also for in-house training and development of self-assessment skills of professional interpreters.

1 Introduction

Computer-assisted interpreter training (CAIT), as a relatively new field in interpreting studies, explores the implementation of information and communication technologies (ICT) in the training of interpreters. Currently very little, if any research has been conducted on CAIT within the South African context. International research on CAIT and its application in the development of self-assessment

Elizabeth Deysel & Harold Lesch. 2018. Experimenting with computer-assisted interpreter training tools for the development of self-assessment skills: National Parliament of RSA. in Claudio Fantinuoli (ed.), *Interpreting and technology*, 61–90. Berlin: Language Science Press. DOI:10.5281/zenodo.1493295

skills has focused mainly on its implementation within institutions of higher learning as a tool in the training of student interpreters. There has been no focus on the possible use in the training and self-assessment of the practicing interpreter. These CAIT tools may also prove useful when utilized for self-assessment skills development within institutions that employ interpreters on a permanent basis.

The curriculum for training interpreters has seen a significant evolution over the past two decades. The implementation of information and communication technologies (ICT) in interpreter training is a useful additional tool in the interpreting curriculum. ICTs provide a variety of tools that can enhance the teaching and learning of interpreting and how trainers go about the process of training potential interpreters. This contention is borne out by the number of scholars who have recently shown an interest in and published texts on the subject. In this regard, the contributions of Lim (2014), Pinazo (2008), Gorm Hansen & Shlesinger (2007), Sandrelli (2005), Lee (2005) and Sandrelli (2015; 2005; 2002) are relevant. The aforementioned studies led to insights that the implementation of computer-assisted interpreter training (CAIT) in the training of interpreters may be desirable and an appropriate addition to traditional training methods as it holds a number of advantages for both the trainee and the trainer. One of the main advantages highlighted in these studies is the shift towards and emphasis on learner autonomy.

The aforementioned studies were conducted within the context of implementation in the interpreting curriculum and the training of student interpreters at institutions of higher learning. However, these tools may also prove useful when utilized by freelance professional interpreters and within institutions that employ professional interpreters on a permanent basis. This study poses the question whether these CAIT tools are effective in the development of self-assessment skills in the professional interpreter. This question was approached by utilizing the CAIT software, *Black Box*[1], within a professional interpreting environment chosen as the Interpreting Unit of the National Parliament of South Africa. The effectiveness of this training software as a self-assessment skills development tool for practicing interpreters was evaluated.

In the context of the latter area of interest, this article presents research conducted on the utilization of CAIT as a tool for the development of self-assessment skills in professional interpreters. The article is organized as follows: firstly, the

---

[1] In 2002, Melissi Multimedia Ltd. (UK) collaborated with the University of Hull (UK) on the design of a digital language laboratory. As part of this development, a dedicated interpreter training module, called *Black Box*, was included. The software *Black Box* was developed as a commercial product by Melissi Ltd. in 2005.

rationale concerning self-assessment and computer-assisted interpreter training is highlighted; secondly, an overview of the methodology is provided; thereafter the results pertaining to the hypotheses are discussed.

2 Theoretical background: Self-assessment and CAIT

In this section, information is provided on self-assessment in interpreting, computer-assisted interpreter training and background on the professional interpreter.

2.1 Self-assessment in interpreting

Regehr et al. (1996: 74) define self-assessment as the ability of each individual to identify his or her own relative strengths and weaknesses. They also offered a reconceptualization of self-assessment that shifted from a focus on the individual's ability to rate themselves relative to their peers and moved on to explore the ability of the individual to identify their own strengths and weaknesses relative to each other. It is suggested that the ability to identify areas of performance that require the greatest degree of improvement would lend greater efficiency to self-directed learning efforts.

Riccardi (2002) states that the training period is of key importance for introducing future interpreters to the habits of recognizing their strengths and weaknesses. Interpreter training courses are intensive in nature and training is complimented by additional self-study hours. However, self-study hours as in the case of experiential learning bear the risk of being of little use if there is no reflection upon the experience. Sandrelli & de Manuel Jerez (2007: 4) state in this regards that "if unsupervised practice sessions are to be useful, students need to be able to assess their own performance and identify their weaknesses. Indeed, the development of self-assessment skills is an essential component of interpreter training".

There is agreement in the research by Pinazo (2008: 197) when contending that the training period is vital for introducing interpreters to self-assessment skills and that the integration of self-assessment skills will also have positive effects on learners' attitudes to self-criticism and performance.

Fowler (2007: 254) emphasizes the importance of self-assessment skills in interpreting when she explains that after training most interpreters remain isolated throughout their professional lives and the process of monitoring is likely to be left to the interpreters themselves. If the interpreter is not self-aware, and has neither skill to be able to assess or evaluate their own performance nor take action to improve upon weaknesses, the service user will suffer the consequences. She elaborates that self-assessment in interpreter training therefore fosters good professional habits in the interpreter. This is also mentioned by Lee (2005: 3) when he states that "self-assessment is not only important during the training phase of interpretation, but it is critical to professional interpreters as well". He further explains that "freelance interpreters are often left to check their own interpretation quality and find measures for improvement" (Lee 2005: 2). The research from Sandrelli & de Manuel Jerez (2007: 15) has also highlighted that "self-assessment skills and the ability to assess other interpreters' performances are essential for trainees, both to ensure progress and to maintain quality standards in their future careers as professional interpreters".

The research conducted on the subject (Riccardi 2002; Lee 2005; Sandrelli & de Manuel Jerez 2007; Fowler 2007; Pinazo 2008) indicates that the development of self-assessment skills is essential in interpreter training. It is concluded that the development of self-assessment skills in the student interpreter will allow for the ability of the individual to recognise his or her strengths and weaknesses and apply appropriate coping mechanisms to enhance the parts of their performance that need improvement. The development of these self-assessment skills will foster good professional habits which can be used to monitor their progress and ensure quality standards in the future career of the professional interpreter.

2.2 Computer-assisted interpreter training

Sandrelli & de Manuel Jerez (2007) indicate that since the 1990s several independent projects were undertaken that shaped the gradual development of what has come to be known as CAIT. This development has resulted in the division of CAIT into what is known as *integrative CAIT* and *intelligent CAIT*. Integrative CAIT entails the implementation of ICT in interpreter training focused on the creation of digital speech repositories in the form of databases, such as the *Interpreters' Information System* (IRIS) developed at the University of Trieste in mid 1990s (Carabelli 1997) and *Marius* developed at the University of Granada in 2001 (Pöchhacker 1994). These projects collected digital training materials and streamlined these resources for use by students in self-study sessions. They have been labelled as *integrative CAIT* – since a project like this "exploits the integration of audio, video and textual resources to provide students with suitable material for classroom use of self-study" (Sandrelli & de Manuel Jerez 2007: 277). On the other hand, *intelligent CAIT* involved the development of authoring programs such as *Interpretations* and *Black Box*, which enables interpreter trainers to create various types of exercises.

4 Experimenting with computer-assisted interpreter training tools

Berber (2010: 229) was one of the first who investigated the use of Information and Communication Technologies in interpreter training and elaborated on the use of these tools as means[2] or pedagogical tools, even though ICT does not facilitate interpreting immediately but enhances learning over time. She also integrated the Effort Model (Gile 1995) and which of the efforts can be backed up by ICT. Berber (2010: 237) concluded that ICTs in general support the efforts presented in the Effort Model and that information technology in the form of interpreter training tools are specifically aimed at the second effort (production) of Gile's Effort Model, where the student can "listen to him/herself repeatedly for self-evaluation and improvement of production skills". In her research, Berber (2010: 243) indicated that the types of ICT which are being used for self-training are mainly traditional: booths, language labs, digital recordings, video and audio recordings, internet, PCs, e-learning platforms.[3]

CAIT tools include CR-ROMs, speech repositories, speech and recording databases and authoring tools such as the software program *Black Box*. The aforementioned software program allows interpreter trainers to create and develop their own set of interpreting exercises for use by individuals and interpreting students in their own time for their self-study sessions. Research that has been conducted on the topic of CAIT (Sandrelli & de Manuel Jerez 2007; Pinazo 2008; Lim 2014) indicates that implementing CAIT in the training of interpreters not only enhances the teaching and learning of interpreting, but also enables the creation of a realistic practice environment in which student interpreters are able to develop their self-assessment skills by listening to their own interpreting and reflect upon it. Bartłomiejczyk (2007: 252) indicates that self-evaluation by means of critically listening to one's own recorded interpreting has often been suggested as a useful method of quality control. The development of self-assessment skills enables the student interpreter to identify strengths and weaknesses, apply appropriate coping strategies and monitor their progress and performance.

In her research, Sandrelli (2005) discusses the development of the interpreter training prototype, *Interpretations*, and how that prototype was improved to become the CAIT authoring tool known as *Black Box*. In 2002, Melissi Multimedia Ltd. (UK) collaborated with the University of Hull (UK) on the design of a digital language laboratory. As part of this development, a dedicated interpreter training module, called *Black Box*, was included. After interest was shown by interpreter training institutions, Melissi Multimedia Ltd decided to develop *Black*

---

[2] The term "means" indicates that the ICT tools are used to practice and develop skills – as opposed to being used for support during or in preparation of actual interpreting.
[3] Specific brands of equipment are X-class, Melissi Black Box, Sanako, Dialang language tests, DEYA lab, Trados, Audacity, BNc online and Brähler.

Box as a stand-alone program, and it was released in March 2005. *Black Box* is an authoring program – this means that the interpreter trainer has complete control over the resources contained within the program. The software was developed with a hierarchy of how materials are structured. There may be different courses and each of these courses may contain different modules, which will then each contain different exercises. The software's authoring function allows the interpreter trainer to create these different courses, modules or exercises, which may comprise simultaneous, consecutive (including liaison interpreting) as well as exercises for sight translation.

The different exercises suggested by the developers are:

a. shadowing and closing

b. paraphrasing

c. sight translation

d. simultaneous interpreting

e. simultaneous interpreting with text

f. consecutive interpreting

Potentially it allows one to compile exercises the way you want them to be, by combining text, video and audio. These are suggested activities that take into account an interpreter's learning path in a specific course. Sandrelli & de Manuel Jerez (2007: 10) also indicated that the *Wizard* makes it possible to add many more resources, including instructions to students, a written translation of the speech, written exercises (comprehension questions, text analysis exercises) and a teacher's interpreted version of the speech. Teachers can also manipulate the sound stream by adding an echo effect or sound distortion in order to simulate realistic working conditions. The source text transcripts can be annotated by adding a hot footnote. Students read the note made by the teacher simply by moving the mouse over the word. In the sight translation exercises the text is presented to students in a scrolling cylinder which advances at the pace established by the teacher.

2.3 The professional interpreter?

Since this research study focused on the utilization of CAIT beyond institutions of higher learning in to interpreting practice, the term "professional interpreter" was often referred to. It was thus deemed necessary to provide a definition of the concept "professional interpreter". Using time as a measure to achieve professional status, in an article by Sandrelli (2015: 115), reference is made to Moser-Mercer (in Motta 2007) who estimates that 3000–5000 hours of deliberate practice are required in order to achieve professional levels of expertise in interpreting. The footnote of the mentioned article indicates that AIIC (International Association of Conference Interpreters), admits new members with a minimum of 150 days of work experience.

In her article on *Language practitioners and standards*, Feinauer (2005: 162) states that the characteristics of a profession are "mastery of a particular skill through education and training, acceptance of duties to a broader society than merely one's clients/employers, objectivity and high standards of conduct and performance". She goes further and defines the profile of a professional as an individual "trained to recognise standards of competence, adheres to a recognised code of practice and enjoys the support and regulation of a professional structure" all the while stating that professionalism is a relative term.

In summary, the term "professional interpreter" is therefore defined as an interpreter presumed to not simply be competent but having mastered their skill with prior experience and/or training in interpreting and adhering to high standards of conduct supported by a code of practice.

3 Methodology

This section provides information regarding the research design, respondents and the methods (questionnaires, experiment and interviews) used to collect the empirical data.

3.1 Research design

Using the above background as the point of departure, the primary objective of the research was to investigate and evaluate the effectiveness of the CAIT software, *Black Box*, in the development of self-assessment skills of professional interpreters in the National Parliament[4] of South Africa. To address the primary

---

[4]The National Parliament of South Africa makes use of interpreting into the eleven official languages during their sittings as well as Sign Language. The eleven official languages are

research objective as stated, the following secondary research questions were explored:

- To what extend does training in self-assessment for interpreters give a better understanding of the strengths and weaknesses of their interpreting?
- To what extend does training in self-assessment for interpreters give a better understanding of the criteria used in the evaluation of interpreting performance?
- What is the correlation of the self-assessment ratings between the experimental group and the ratings from the expert assessor post-experiment?
- What is the correlation of the self-assessment ratings between the control group when compared to the experimental group post-experiment?

The research design most suitable for this study comprised an evaluation study approach, based on an experimental intervention design, i.e. a type of study in which participants are assigned to groups that receive one or other intervention or no intervention so that the effects of the intervention can be evaluated. An intervention research includes studies in which researches follow a systematic change in the condition to determine the effects on a physical capacity, skill or performance. In the evaluation of the effectiveness of the CAIT software, *Black Box*, the software was utilized as an intervention in the form of technological innovation in voluntary in-house training to support professional interpreters in their professional development. It should be noted here that the in-house training formed part of this research study and was not initiated or permanently implemented by the Parliament of South Africa. Therefore, the researchers' personal PC was used in the sessions which has one licensed copy of *Black Box*. The participants were exposed to self-assessment sessions on *Black Box* in individual sessions where they received the same brief and instructions beforehand. The sessions were conducted during lunch hours in a sound-proof room with two sound-proof doors.

The empirical study sought to obtain quantitative and qualitative data. This meant that the core method was of a quantitative nature, while the supplementary method was of a qualitative nature, and was used to extend the findings of the quantitative data. The quantitative data was collected from the experiment, which required the interpreters to complete self-assessment grids (see Appendix)

Afrikaans, English, isiNdebele, isiXhosa, isiZulu, Sepedi, Sesotho, Setswana, siSwati, Tshivenda, Xitsonga.

in both the control and experimental groups. An investigation by means of a questionnaire (see Appendix A) and interviews (see Appendix B) formed part of the qualitative follow-up to investigate the outcomes from the quantitative data.

It should be emphasized that this is a pilot study as the sample size of respondents is extremely small and may contribute to the data not being statistically significant. To put this into context the following background information should be noted.

According to Human Resources of National Parliament of South Africa (Moorad 2017), 38 language practitioners were employed within the Interpreting Unit at the time of conducting this study. Of these 38 practitioners, three were Sign Language interpreters. These interpreters could not participate in the study, as the software, *Black Box*, does not make provision for video recording. This left 35 language practitioners available for participation in the study.

The institutional permission the researcher received from Parliament to conduct the research within the Interpreting Unit stipulated that data may only be collected outside of work hours. The researcher agreed to this stipulation, which meant the lunch hour was used for data collection. The experimental part of the study – that involved the self-training sessions on *Black Box* – would take up to 30 minutes per person per session. With the time allocation for the experiment in mind, the researcher calculated that only five respondents per week could form part of the experiment. A limitation resulting from this agreement is that the researcher observed that collecting data from participants outside of working hours i.e. during their lunch breaks, may discourage some respondents from participating in the study and that reluctance may result in the entire population in the unit of analysis not participating in the data collection.

When surveying only a sample of the population, researchers have to consider margins of error and confidence levels of the data that is collected: the margin of error is the amount of error which can be tolerated, while the confidence level is the amount of uncertainty that can be tolerated. The margin of error for this study was set at 25% while the confidence level in the study was set at 90%. Given the population of 35 possible respondents, the sample size was calculated at nine.

For this study, it was decided that anything above 26% as a margin of error would be too high. A margin of error of 25.91% would mean that eight respondents would form part of the study. The researcher had to bear the possibility of discouragement of some respondents in mind, and thus decided to send the questionnaire to double the amount, resulting in 16 interpreters receiving the link to the questionnaire. Only ten of the 16 respondents had completed the questionnaire.

The experimental method in this study involved:

- selecting a group of respondents[5] who fit into the category of 'professional interpreter'
- dividing them into an experimental group and a control group using the quota matching method
- exposing the experimental group to a stimulus – in this case four self-assessment sessions on *Black Box*
- observing and measuring the effect of the stimulus on the respondents. The experiment itself entailed pre- and post-testing of the respondents. The pre-testing tested the respondents to determine their self-assessment skills

The experimental group was then exposed to self-assessment sessions which served as the intervention. Finally, post-testing was conducted to determine if the intervention had any impact on the development of self-assessment skills of the interpreters.

3.2 Respondents

A sample representative of the population deemed as 'professional interpreters' according to the above stated definition was selected as the unit of analysis for the research. For the purpose of the study, the term 'professional interpreter' was defined as an interpreter presumed to not simply be competent but having mastered their skill with prior experience and/or training in interpreting and adhering to high standards of conduct supported by a code of practice. Interpreters who, at the time of the study, were employed full-time within the Interpreting Unit of the Language Services Section at the National Parliament of the Republic of South Africa were chosen as the sample population for this study.[6] A week

---

[5] The necessary ethical clearance was provided from Stellenbosch University as well as institutional clearance from the Parliament of SA. The National Health Research Ethics Committee (NHREC) registration number is REC-050411-032.

[6] Regarding the recruitment policy of parliament for interpreters, it is suffice to state here that as there is relative short history of interpreting, interpreters were initially recruited from the teaching profession. However, over the last couple of years some inroads have been made as trained interpreters were appointed. These interpreters currently provide for all the 11 official languages as well Sign Language. Please see Lesch (2010) for information on recruitment and training of parliamentary interpreters.

after the link to the questionnaire was sent out via email, ten of the interpreters in the Unit completed the questionnaire and were subsequently divided into the control group (5 respondents) and the experimental group (5 respondents) using the quota matching method. The characteristics which were used to divide the respondents equally into the two different groups were:

1. working languages
2. interpreting education and/or training
3. experience in interpreting

3.3 The questionnaire

The questionnaire was divided into different sections, all of which aimed to collect data on:

- the biographical details of the respondents pertaining to their experience and education in interpreting
- the perceived knowledge of the respondents as pertaining to their self-assessment activities and their awareness of his/her strengths and weaknesses in interpreting performance
- the respondents' perceived knowledge about the evaluation process and the applicable criteria considered when evaluating an interpreting performance

A copy of the questionnaire in its entirety is included in Appendix A. The main section is discussed:

Question 1 of the questionnaire dealt with the working languages of the interpreters and the researchers asked the question to determine the working languages. The majority (80%) of the respondents indicated that they provide interpreting in English.[7] The data for the Language A[8] distribution was indicated as Afrikaans (20%), isiZulu (20%), SiSwati (20%), isiNdebele (10%), Sepedi (10%), Sesotho (10%) and Tshivenda (10%).

---

[7] Although only 80% of the respondents indicated they deliver interpreting services in English, it forms part of the employment contract of the interpreters in Parliament that they must all be able to interpret into English as their B language.

[8] Language A is representative of the respondents' mother tongue or first language.

Questions 2, 4 and 5 of the questionnaire dealt with the interpreters' practical experience in interpreting. The questions sought to determine how many years' experience the interpreter had, if the interpreter had any experience in interpreting before they started interpreting at Parliament and lastly in what setting (e.g. court, health care, conference), the interpreter had experience. The majority (40%) of the respondents indicated they had between 5–9 years' experience as an interpreter, followed by 30% indicating they have between 10–20 years' experience as an interpreter. Two respondents (20%) indicated that they had less than 5 years' experience while only one respondent (10%) indicated that they had more than 21 years' experience in interpreting.

In question 4, the majority (70%) of the respondents had indicated that they had prior experience in interpreting before they started interpreting at Parliament.

Question 5 was an open-ended question inquiring as to the setting where the respondent had provided interpreting services. All 7 respondents who had indicated prior experience responded to the question and the text responses were categorized as follow; three interpreters indicated that they had conference interpreting experience. This included interpreting for the Truth and Reconciliation Commission, Provincial Legislature, conferences, general meetings and workshops. Two interpreters indicated that they had court interpreting experience. One interpreter indicated they had experience in educational interpreting at university. One interpreter indicated that they had their own company which provided interpreting services, while another interpreter had indicated that they had been working as a freelance interpreter for 4 years. In both these instances the specific setting where interpreting services were rendered was not provided.

Question 3 dealt with the interpreters' employment at Parliament. The researchers wanted to determine how many years the interpreter had been interpreting in the environment of the Parliament. This data would also indicate how experienced the interpreter is in conference interpreting particularly with Parliamentary speeches and terminology. The responses indicated that 50% of the respondents had been working as an interpreter in Parliament for 5–9 years. 20% had been working for 10–20 years and 30% had been working for less than 5 years.

The majority (80%) of the respondents indicated that they held a qualification in interpreting, translation or a language practitioner related qualification. Of these, four indicated that they held a tertiary diploma; one indicated a Bachelor's degree and three indicated that they held an Honours degree, i.e. a qualification after the BA degree that gives access to study on Masters level. The majority (60%) of the respondents indicated that they received informal training. The informal training was listed as in-house training and short courses.

3.4 Data collection

The data collected from the biographical information in the questionnaires was used in the quota matrix matching method from experimental studies to divide the respondents equally into the control group (five respondents) and the experimental group (five respondents). A quota sampling method entails gathering representative data from a group. As opposed to random sampling, quota sampling requires that the individuals are chosen out of a specific subgroup.

The respondents were all coded by using letters of the alphabet (A–J) and the data obtained from the biographical information pertaining to prior experience and education in interpreting were then tabulated according to these codes and the matching method was used to divide the respondents on a random basis equally into two groups; namely the experimental group that will be exposed to training, and the control group that won't receive any training.

Table 1: Matching method division of respondents

	2 Experience	4 Prior Experience	5 Setting	6 Qualification	7 Type of Qualification	8 Informal training	9 Type of training
A	21+	Yes	TRC	No		No	
B	1–5	No		Yes	Hons.	Yes	In-house
C	10–20	No		Yes	Postgraduate Diploma	Yes	In-house
D	5–9	Yes	Church	No		No	
E	5–9	Yes	Freelance	Yes	Postgraduate Diploma	Yes	In-house
F	10–20	Yes	Freelance	Yes	Bachelors	Yes	Practical
G	5–9	Yes	Church	Yes	Hons.	No	
H	1–5	No		Yes	Diploma	Yes	Short Course
I	10–20	Yes	Court/ Conferences	Yes	Postgraduate Diploma	Yes	In-house
J	5–9	Yes	University/ Legislature	Yes	Hons.	Yes	In-house

The second part of the data collection was the experiment itself. The experiment comprised three major pairs of components:

1. independent (*Black Box*) and dependent variables (self-assessment skills)

2. pre-testing and post-testing

3. experimental (participate in four self-training sessions on *Black Box*) and control groups

Table 2: Experimental group and Control Group

Experimental Group	Control Group
B	A
C	E
D	F
G	H
I	J

The experimental stimulus, *Black Box*, was administered to the experimental group over a course of four sessions. The respondents from the experimental group were required to complete four self-assessment sessions of between 30–60 minutes each (consisting of 10–13 minutes introduction and interpreting exercise itself; 12–15 minutes listening to the recording of target and source speech and finally 13–16 minutes completion of the self-assessment grid). The self-training sessions consisted of one simultaneous interpreting exercise on the software *Black Box*, where a parliamentary speech of between 6 and 8 minutes had to be interpreted. The speech was made up of a video as well as audio clip. The target (interpretation of respondent) and source (original text) speeches of the self-assessment sessions were recorded on *Black Box* which compresses the target and source speech into one single audio file. After completing the interpreting exercise, respondents were required to listen to the recording and use a provided grid for self-assessment. The self-assessment grids were collected after each respondent had completed it. The aggregate out of 15 for each session was recorded to track progress and compare the marks from each session.

The ten respondents who participated in the experiment interpreted into their A language, i.e. 7 different languages which formed part of the experimental output. As indicated in §3.3, the data for the Language A distribution was indicated as Afrikaans (20%), isiZulu (20%), SiSwati (20%), isiNdebele (10%), Sepedi (10%), Sesotho (10%) and Tshivenda (10%). An expert for each of these languages was utilized to conduct the expert rating. These experts are rated on their seniority in terms of their language specific background but also their interpreting experience as well as the in-house principles that applied in Parliament. They made use of the same assessment grid as utilised by the participants and as attached in the Appendix .

The video material used in the self-assessment interpreting sessions was recorded during National Parliamentary sittings of the National Assembly, readily

4 Experimenting with computer-assisted interpreter training tools

available on the National Parliament of the Republic of South Africa's YouTube channel. The video material consisted of four speeches from different debates and different political parties, and the length varied from 6 to 8 minutes. The dominant language spoken in the recordings was English, but session 2 contained some Setswana and isiNdebele and session 4 contained some isiZulu. Table 3 below is a representation of the four different sessions.

Table 3: Summary of the different interpreting sessions

	Session 1	Session 2	Session 3	Session 4
Language(s)	English	English Setswana isiNdebele	English	English isiZulu
Topic	Debate on the State of the Nation 2016	Question Session	Debate on the State of the Nation 2016	Debate on the Marikana Commission of Inquiry
Duration	6:35min	7:45min	7:47min	6:35min

For the first self-assessment session on *Black Box* the respondents allocated a mark for pre-testing, i.e. before the intervention. In the final self-assessment session the respondents in the experiment allocated a mark that represents their post-testing mark.

In a traditional experiment the control group is never exposed to the stimulus. However, for this research the only way of obtaining a recording which was similar to that of the experimental group was for the control group to be exposed to the stimulus. The pre- and post-testing for the control group was done using the same instrument, *Black Box*, which was the experimental stimulus in this study. Thus, unlike a traditional experiment in which the control group is never exposed to the stimulus, the control group in this experiment received exposure to the stimulus as they had to complete one session of self-assessment of interpreting performance on *Black Box* in order to get their interpreting assessment score. This was done by allowing the control group to listen to both the target and source texts and to conduct self-assessment. Self-assessment does not necessarily require one to listen to the recording, however in this case it was expected from interpreters to listen to it and reflect on it for self-assessment. The mark obtained in the one session completed on *Black Box* by the control group was used as data for pre- and post-testing. Thus, the comparison between the two groups includes the fact that the experimental group received exposure and training on

Black Box over four sessions, whereas the control group only had one session on *Black Box*.

At the end of the four sessions, the respondents from the experimental group were interviewed, which aimed to extend the findings of the quantitative data. The main aim of having the interviews was to conduct a follow-up and evaluate the perceptions of the respondents regarding their strengths and weaknesses as well as the criteria they used when evaluating interpreting performance post-experiment. The interviews were structured and based on written questions (see Appendix B) and were conducted individually after the respondents from the experimental group completed their final self-assessment session.

4 Results

Hypothesis testing was used to analyze the quantitative data obtained from the experiment. In hypothesis testing two opposing hypotheses are measured. The two hypotheses are known as the null hypothesis and the alternative hypothesis. The alternative hypothesis is based on the aim of the research, in other words, that the observed differences are the result of real effects, while the null hypothesis would state that there is no significant difference between the populations specified by the study. In hypothesis testing, the null hypothesis is assumed to be true. In this instance, the null hypothesis would be that there is no difference between the means from the absolute errors pre- and post-experiment from the experimental group. The alpha of 0.05 is used as a guideline to determine to what extent the hypothesis may be accepted or rejected. In most analyses, an alpha of 0.05 is used as the cut-off for significance. If the p-value is less than 0.05 ($p < 0.05$), the null hypothesis is rejected. If the p-value is larger than 0.05 ($p > 0.05$) the null hypothesis is accepted to be true.

Against this background the hypothesis regarding the effectiveness of training software as a self-assessment skills development tool for practicing interpreters is evaluated.

4.1 Was there a difference in the correlation of self-assessment ratings from the experimental group and the ratings from the expert assessor post-experiment?

As hypothesis testing was used to analyze the quantitative data obtained from the experiment, the hypothesis test was set up to determine the validity of the statistical claim that there was no difference between the absolute error means pre- and post-experiment. The p-value from the experimental data was calculated at 0.24198 (see Figure 1), which meant that based on the p-value, a significant difference could not be concluded. Alternatively, it can be stated as in Table 4.

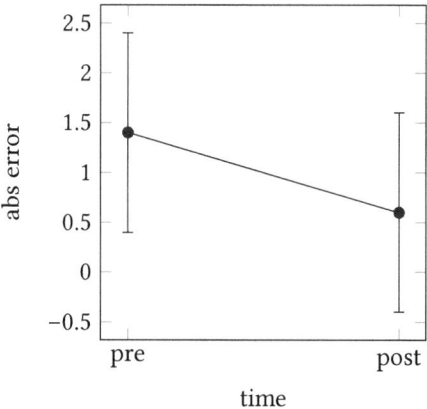

Figure 1: Means of absolute errors pre-experiment and post-experiment

Table 4: Descriptive statistics for hypothesis testing

	Descriptive statistics		
Effect	Level of factor	Number	Absolute error mean
Total		10	1.00
Time	Pre	5	1.40
Time	Post	5	0.60

Although the results were not statistically significant, the descriptive statistics did indicate that over time the experimental group's absolute error mean ratings did decrease (see Table 4). The decreasing absolute error indicates that after exposure to the experiment there were more self-ratings which corresponded with the rating from the experts. The comparison of pre-experimental and post-experimental data (see Table 5) pertaining to the self-ratings and expert-ratings from the experimental group indicated that, pre-experiment, only one respondent could accurately rate themselves in accordance with the rating by the experts. However, there may be shortcomings as this is a small-scale experiment and data was only collected at two instances. Post-experiment data indicated that three respondents could accurately rate themselves in accordance with the rating by the experts.

Table 5: Experimental group ratings pre- and post-experiment

Experimental Group					
Pre-experiment			Post-experiment		
Self-rating (out of 15)	Expert Rating (out of 15)	Difference	Self-rating (out of 15)	Expert Rating (out of 15)	Difference
11	11	0	12	12	0
9	12	3	11	11	0
12	11	−1	12	12	0
13	12	−1	13	12	−1
13	11	−2	13	11	−2

4.2 Was there a difference in the self-assessment ratings of the control group when compared to the experimental group post-experiment?

The means between the final sessions from the experimental group and the control group (see Table 6) did indicate a difference, with the experimental group scoring higher ratings overall. The experimental group's average final self-assessment ratings were calculated as a mark of 12.2 out of 15, and the average final self-assessment rating from the control group was calculated as a mark of 10.8 out of 15. However, since the control group only had one set of ratings – it could not be used for statistical analysis. The possibility exists that there are other variables which may have contributed to the difference in ratings.

4.3 Do the self-assessment sessions give the interpreters a better awareness of their strengths and weaknesses in interpreting?

The analysis of the qualitative data from the questionnaire indicated that it was the perception of the majority of respondents that their strengths in interpreting far outweigh their weaknesses. The qualitative data from Question 11 (*How often do you struggle with the following challenges in interpreting?*) indicated that it was the perception of the majority of the respondents (80%) that they seldom struggled with challenges in interpreting.

The qualitative data from Question 12 (*Indicate your ability with regard to the following in simultaneous interpreting*) indicated that there was a positive perception among the majority of respondents when asked a negative Likert-scale question; for example, when the question was posed in the negative, the majority

4 Experimenting with computer-assisted interpreter training tools

Table 6: Comparison of ratings for experimental and control group

Experimental Group Post-experiment			Control Group Post-experiment		
Self-rating	Expert Rating	Difference	Self-rating	Expert Rating	Difference
12	12	0	12	12	0
11	11	0	12	9	−3
12	12	0	7	8	1
13	12	−1	13	12	−1
13	11	−2	10	9	−1
Averages of groups					
12.2	11.6		10.8	10	

of answers were found among the choices of "*never*" and "*seldom*". When posed with a positive question, the majority of the answers were "*frequently*" and "*always*". It was seldom that a respondent indicated a challenge or weakness in their interpreting performance.

The marks obtained, both the self-assessment rating as well as the ratings from the experts, in the self-assessment grids from the experimental group respondents were high (see Table 6). However, the specific questions posed under each macro error section of the self-assessment grids showed that the respondents did encounter challenges in their interpreting performance, especially when it pertained to the interpretation of idiomatic expressions and accurate interpretation of numbers and dates.

In the qualitative data from the interviews, it was the perception of all respondents that the self-training sessions gave them a better awareness of their strengths and weaknesses. In answer to Q3 (*Were you satisfied with your interpreting performance?*), four of the respondents were satisfied with their interpreting performance and one respondent indicated that they were "not quite" satisfied. In answer to Q4 (*Was your interpreting performance better or worse than you expected?*), all the respondents indicated that their performance was better than they had expected. In answer to Q5 (*In the questionnaire there was a section pertaining to your abilities in interpreting. After having conducted self-assessment – do you think that your initial judgments were correct?*), two of the respondents indicated that their initial judgments of their abilities in interpreting had been correct. One respondent indicated that their ability was better than they had expected. Other respondents indicated that their judgments were correct but that they "*can do better of course*". One respondent indicated that "*some things were* better than I thought they would be". In answer to Q14 (*Do you feel that the self-study sessions has given you a better awareness of your strengths and weaknesses in interpreting?*), all respondents indicated that the self-assessment session gave them a better awareness of their strengths and weaknesses.

4.4 Do the self-assessment sessions give the interpreters a better awareness of the criteria used in the evaluation of interpreting performance?

The data collected from the questionnaires indicated that the perception of the respondents regarding the criteria used in the evaluation of interpreting performance was quite vague and incomplete. Question 13 of the questionnaire is an open-ended question inquiring from the respondents to list the criteria they find important in the evaluation of an interpreting performance. The data collected from this question was arranged in tabular format according to the macro errors; 1) accuracy, 2) target language and 3) delivery (see Figure 2; also see Appendix again). Under each of the macro errors examples of errors were listed. A heading for 'other' was been added. From the data provided, it was deduced that the respondents were not completely aware of the criteria used when evaluating an interpreting performance. Only half of the respondents (50%) indicated that accuracy is important in the evaluation of interpreting performance, while only 20% of respondents indicated that target language is important in the evaluation of interpreting performance. The majority of examples listed by the respondents were found under the macro error of delivery. However, each respondent listed only one item under this macro error.

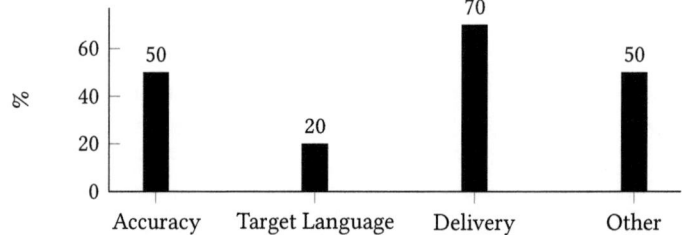

Figure 2: Criteria used for evaluation of interpreting performance: Distribution of perceptions of respondents

The data collected and analyzed for the macro error of accuracy indicate that it is the perception of half of the respondents (50%) that accuracy is important in the evaluation of interpreting performance. The terms "accuracy", "content accuracy" and "message accuracy" were used. None of the respondents list "omissions" or "additions" as criteria. There were also no examples given of what constitutes "accuracy".

The data analyzed for target language indicate that it is the perception of 20% of respondents that target language is important in the evaluation of interpreting performance. Only two respondents (20%) listed criteria pertaining to the category of target language by indicating that 'terminology accuracy' and 'vocabulary' are important criteria in the evaluation of interpreting performance. One respondent (10%) indicated that 'sentence construction' is important when evaluating interpreting performance.

In the analysis of the data under the macro error of delivery, seven respondents (70%) listed criteria which pertain to delivery. Eleven different micro errors were listed as criteria important in the evaluation of interpreting performance. The analysis of data gathered from this question reveals a strong focus on the macro error of delivery when seen in relation to the variety of micro errors listed. Two respondents (20%) listed the micro error pertaining to tone of voice by stating: 'tone of voice follows the speaker' and 'voice tone'. Two respondents (20%) listed criteria pertaining to the micro error of audibility by listing: 'audibility'.

Eleven other micro errors pertaining to the category of delivery were listed; Absence of fillers – 10%; Avoiding long pauses – 10%; Breathing – 10%; Consistency – 10%; Coherence – 10%; Correct intonation – 10%; Delivery smooth and clear – 10%; Pleasant to hear presentation – 10%; Time lag 10%. Only one respondent (10%) listed criteria across all three different macro errors (accuracy, target language, delivery).

In the qualitative data from the interviews, it was the perception of all respondents that the exposure to the self-assessment sessions had improved their understanding of the criteria used in the evaluation of an interpreting performance. In answer to Q6 (*Before the self-study sessions – were you aware of criteria used in the evaluation of interpreting?*), two of the respondents indicated that, before the self-assessment sessions, they were not aware of the criteria used in the evaluation of interpreting. Three respondents indicated that they were aware of the criteria used in the evaluation of interpreting. In answer to Q7 (*Do you feel that your understanding of the criteria has improved with the self-study sessions?*) when asked if the respondents' understanding of the criteria had improved with the exposure to the self-assessment sessions, there was a consensus among all five respondents that their understanding had improved. One respondent indicated that their understanding of the criteria improved, especially after completing the electronic questionnaire. The questions posed in the questionnaire might have triggered the respondents' thoughts and lead them to reflect on the criteria used when evaluating interpreting performance. The self-assessment grids which were used in the self-assessment session also clearly indicated the various macro errors and criteria used for the evaluation of an interpreting session.

5 Conclusion

It is important to emphasize that the study did not seek to evaluate the performance of the interpreters but it was rather aimed at evaluating self-assessment skills of the interpreters. The marks from both the self-assessment and expert ratings were relatively high – indicating that the interpreters perform at a high level. This ought to be expected since the interpreters are no longer student interpreters, but full-time professional interpreters. The means (both the self-ratings and the ratings by the experts) between the final sessions from the experimental group and the control group did indicate a difference in the averages from the groups (see Table 6), with the experimental group scoring higher ratings. This indicates that their self-assessment did differ from that of the control group. However, there are several variables which may have contributed to this difference in ratings.

The empirical study sought to obtain quantitative and qualitative data. The primary research aim of the study set out to evaluate whether the CAIT tool, *Black Box*, was effective in the development of self-assessment skills in professional interpreters. The primary research aim was sub-divided into four research questions and that was addressed above under the results. According to the results of this small scale research study, it can be concluded that the CAIT tool, *Black Box*, may prove effective in the development of self-assessment skills in professional interpreters.

Appendix A: An example of the self-assessment grid

SELF-ASSESSMENT SHEET					
Debate on the State of the Nation Address					
Duration: 6:35min					
Read through all the questions in this self-assessment sheet before you start with the playback of the recording. You are allowed to pause, rewind and make notes while listening to the recording.					
PARTICIPANT CODE:					
1. ACCURACY / CONTENT OF MESSAGE:	1	2	3	4	5
Omissions, Additions, Accuracy *The interpreter must convey the message in a complete, correct and intelligible manner in the target language.*					
1.1 Was important information omitted in this interpreting session?			YES		NO
2. TARGET LANGUAGE	1	2	3	4	5
Vocabulary, Sentence Construction, Idiomatic language use, Grammar *The interpreter must always use the most appropriate vocabulary and be loyal to the register of the speaker.*					
2.1 The following idiomatic language was used in the speech • write down how each statement was interpreted • comment on whether the phrase was interpreted into idiomatic target language					
[00:20mins] "**anxious coin tossing**"					
[1:40mins] "He spoke a lot today about iron and steel. Well, let me tell you something: When it comes to the ANC, **they iron over the problems and steal all the money**."					
3. DELIVERY / COHERENCE / TECHNIQUES and PRESENTATION	1	2	3	4	5
Inarticulate speech, Pauses and hesitations, Audibility, Fillers *The interpreter must maintain sufficient speed to convey the full message of the speaker, employing mechanisms to cope with various complexities, remaining clear and concise.*					
3.1 Is the interpreting audible / clear?			YES		NO
3.2 Are there any fillers (uhm, ah)?			YES		NO
3.3 Are there any unfinished sentences?			YES		NO
3.4 Are there any strange noises (coughing, sighing, heavy breathing)?			YES		NO
3.5 Is the intonation natural or monotonous?			NAT.		MON.
3.6 Is the lag-time managed well?			YES		NO
TOTAL MARK:					/ 15

Appendix B: Questionnaire

INTERPRETING QUESTIONNAIRE

Thank you for taking part in this study! This questionnaire is completed anonymously.

Section A: Interpreting Experience

1	In what language(s) do you provide interpreting?

2	How many years' experience do you have as an interpreter?

21 + years	10–20 years	5–9 Years	Less than 5 years

3	How long have you been employed as an interpreter in Parliament?

21 + years	10–20 years	5–9 Years	Less than 5 years

4	Did you have experience in interpreting before you started working at Parliament?

Yes	No

5	If yes, please specify where you have rendered interpreting services (example; court, clinic, any other):

6	Do you hold a qualification in interpreting/ translation or language practice?

Yes	No

7	If yes, what qualification do you hold?

Diploma	Bachelors	Masters	Honours	PhD

Other, please specify:

8	Have you received any informal interpreter training?

Yes	No

9	If yes, please specify what type of training you received (example; short courses, in-house training, any other):

Section B: Self-assessment activities

10	How often do you...					
		Never	Seldom	Frequently	Always	N/A
10.1	Record your interpreting sessions					
10.2	Listen to recordings of your interpreting sessions					
10.3	Take note of terminology which is challenging in an interpreting session					
10.4	Take note of challenges presented in an interpreting session					
10.5	Conduct self-assessment on an interpreting performance					

Section C: Interpreting strengths and weaknesses

11	How often do you struggle with the following challenges in interpreting?					
		Never	Seldom	Frequently	Always	N/A
11.1	Interpreting proper names					
11.2	Interpreting numbers and figures					
11.3	Interpreting dates					
11.4	Understanding the speakers' accent					
11.5	Following the speakers' speed					

12	Indicate your ability with regards to the following in simultaneous interpreting:					
		Never	Seldom	Frequently	Always	N/A
12.1	I struggle to provide an accurate message					
12.2	I pause within the middle of a sentence					
12.3	I struggle with target language register					

		Never	Seldom	Frequently	Always	N/A
12.4	I struggle with target language terminology					
12.5	I hesitate					
12.6	I have a monotonous intonation					
12.7	I use filler words such as uhm and ah within a sentence					
12.8	My speech is unclear					
12.9	I struggle with target language grammar					
12.10	My target language use is unidiomatic					
12.11	I omit information					
12.12	I add information					
12.13	I do not finish sentences					
12.14	My message delivery is incoherent					
12.15	I struggle with microphone use					
12.16	I need to improve my simultaneous interpreting technique					
12.17	I struggle to concentrate while interpreting					
12.18	I speak too fast					
12.19	I breathe loud					
12.20	I get emotionally involved					
12.21	My delivery is smooth and flows with ease					
12.22	I convey the message accurately					
12.23	I do not make irritating noises					
12.24	My voice sounds pleasant					
12.25	I use the appropriate terminology					
12.26	I do not stop in the middle of a sentence					

Section D: Evaluation of Interpreting Performance

13 List the criteria which you find important in the evaluation of an interpreting performance:

14 Define each of the following macro errors when used to evaluate interpreting performance:

14.1 Accuracy

14.2 Delivery

14.3 Target Language Quality

15 Provide examples of errors according to the following macro errors (for example; accuracy = omissions):

15.1 Accuracy

15.2 Delivery

15.3 Target Language Quality

15 Do you have any other comments?

Appendix C: Interview questions

Q1: Was this the first time you recorded your interpreting performance?

Q2: Was this the first time you listened to yourself interpreting?

Q3: Were you satisfied with your interpreting performance?

Q4: Was your interpreting performance better or worse than you expected?

Q5: In the questionnaire there was a section pertaining to your abilities in interpreting. After having conducted self-assessment – do you think that your initial judgements were correct?

Q6: Before the self-study sessions – were you aware of criteria used in the evaluation of interpreting?

Q7: Do you feel that your understanding of the criteria has improved with the self-study sessions?

Q8: In your first self-study session and self-assessment did you find it difficult to assess yourself?

Q9: Do you feel that the self-study sessions have developed your self-assessment skills?

Q10: Do you feel that it is easier being assessed on your interpreting performance by someone else?

Q11: Do you think that if someone was to assess this very same assessment that you would receive the very same mark?

Q12: Did you find the self-study sessions useful in order to conduct self-assessment?

Q13: Did you find the self-assessment grids useful in your self-assessment?

Q14: Do you feel that the self-study sessions have given you a better awareness of your strengths and weaknesses in interpreting?

Q15: Do you feel that the self-study sessions have improved your interpreting performance?

Q16: What did you find most useful in the self-study sessions?

Q17: Do you feel that the self-study sessions have made you more confident in conducting self-assessment on your interpreting performance?

Q18: Do you have any other comments?

References

Bartłomiejczyk, Magdalena. 2007. Interpreting quality as perceived by trainee interpreters. *The Interpreter and Translator Trainer* 1(2). 247–267.

Berber, Diana-Cristina. 2010. The use of pedagogical and non-pedagogical ICT in conference interpreter training. In V. Pellat, K. Griffiths & W. Shao-Chuan (eds.), *Teaching and testing interpreting and translating*, 229–249. Bern: Peter Lang.

Carabelli, Angela. 1997. IRIS interprerers' resource information system. Una banca dati interattiva per la formazione di interpreti e traduttori. Unpublished dissertation.

Feinauer, A. E. 2005. Language practitioners and standards. In SATI (South African Translators' Institute) (ed.), *Rights in practice*, 162–163. Pretoria: Content Solutions.

Fowler, Yvonne. 2007. Formative assessment: Using peer and self-assessment in interpreter training. In Cecilia Wadensjö, Birgitta Englund Dimitrova & A. L. Nilsson (eds.), *The critical link 4*, 253–262. Amsterdam/Philadelphia: John Benjamins.

Gile, Daniel. 1995. *Basic concepts and models for interpreter and translator training*. Amsterdam/Philadelphia: John Benjamins.

Gorm Hansen, Inge & Miriam Shlesinger. 2007. The silver lining: Technology and self-study in the interpreting classroom. *Interpreting* 9(1). 95–118.

Lee, Yun-Hyang. 2005. Self-assessment as an autonomous learning tool in an interprctation classroom. *Meta* 50(4).

Lesch, Harold. 2010. A descriptive overview of the interpreting service in parliament. *Acta Academica* 42(3). 38–60.

Lim, Lily. 2014. Examining students' perceptions of computer-assisted interpreter training. *The Interpreter and Translator Trainer* 7(1). 71–89.

Moorad, I. 2017. *Staff complement of interpreting unit.* e-mail to E. Deysel, Online, 20 January 2017.

Motta, Manuela. 2007. Evaluation of a blended tutoring program in conference interpreting. In T. Bastiaens & S. Carliner (eds.), *Proceedings of E-Learn: World Conference on E-Learning in Corporate, Government, Healthcare, and Higher Education*, 399–404. Chesapeake, VA: Association for the Advancement of Computing in Education (AACE).

Pinazo, E. Postigo. 2008. Self-assessment in teaching interpreting. *TTR: traduction, termonologie, redaction* 21(1). 173–209.

Pöchhacker, Franz. 1994. *Simultandolmetschen als komlpexes Handeln*. Tübingen: Gunter Narr.

Regehr, Glenn, Brian Hodges, Richard Tiberius & Jdoy Lefchy. 1996. Measuring self-assessment skills: An innovative relative ranking model. *Academic Medicine* 71(10). S52–S74.

Riccardi, Alessandra. 2002. Evaluation in interpretation: Macro-criteria and micro-criteria. In Eva Hung (ed.), *Teaching translation and interpreting 4: Building bridges*, 115–126. Amsterdam/Philadelphia: John Benjamins.

Sandrelli, Annalisa. 2002. Computers in the training of interpreters: Curriculum design issues. In G. Garzone, M. Viezzi & P. Mead (eds.), *Perspectives on interpreting*, 189–204. Bologna: CLUEB.

Sandrelli, Annalisa. 2005. Designing CAIT (computer-assisted interpreter training) tools: Black Box. In Sandra Nauert (ed.), *Challenges of multidimensional translation, Proceedings of the Marie Curie Euroconferences. MuTra: Challenges of multidimensional translation*. Saarbrücken.

Sandrelli, Annalisa. 2015. Becoming an interpreter: The role of computer technology. *MonTI* Special Issue 2. 111–138.

Sandrelli, Annalisa & Jesús de Manuel Jerez. 2007. The impact of information and communication technology on interpreter training: State of the art and future prospects. *The Interpreter and Translator Trainer* 1(2). 269–303.

Chapter 5

Technologies and role-space: How videoconference interpreting affects the court interpreter's perception of her role

Jerome Devaux
The Open University

> Back in 2000, videoconference systems were introduced in criminal courts in England and Wales so that defendants could attend their pre-trial court hearings from prison. Since then, the number of cases heard via videoconference interpreting technologies has been on the increase. In order to be able to conduct a hearing remotely, courts and prisons are equipped with cameras, screens, microphones, and loud-speakers which link up both locations so that participants can hear and see each other. In terms of research, various reports on the viability of such systems acknowledge the benefits of conducting court hearings remotely, whilst also highlighting shortfalls. Interestingly, most of these studies were carried out in a monolingual setting, and fewer studies examine the impact of videoconference interpreting equipment in multilingual court settings. In this context the interpreter's role, and more particularly her role perception when technologies are used in a courtroom, remains under-explored. This paper will demonstrate that, unlike in face-to-face court hearings, technologies force some interpreters to create split role models.

1 Introduction

Since the late 1990s, videoconference (vc) systems have been used in criminal courts in the UK (Plotnikoff & Woolfson 1999; 2000) as a means to reduce cost, enhance security, and speed up proceedings. According to (Braun et al. 2016), 90% of Magistrate's Courts and all Crown Courts were equipped in 2013 with the necessary Videoconference Interpreting (VCI) equipment to enable courts to establish an audio and video feed between the participants physically present in

Jerome Devaux. 2018. Technologies and role-space: How videoconference interpreting affects the court interpreter's perception of her role. In Claudio Fantinuoli (ed.), *Interpreting and technology*, 91–117. Berlin: Language Science Press. DOI:10.5281/zenodo.1493297

a courtroom and the defendant or witness attending from a remote location. In other words, defendants can attend their own court hearing without leaving the prison where they are incarcerated.

Such systems are also used in multilingual court hearings in the UK. In this context, the interpreter can be co-located with the participants in court or with the remote defendant or witness. Braun (2011) makes a useful distinction by referring to VCI A, where the interpreter is in the courtroom and VCI B, where the interpreter is co-located with the remote defendant or witness.

Research in the use of VCI systems in courts dates back to the 1990s and was characterised by its primary focus on monolingual court settings. More recently, the valuable studies carried out as part of the Avidicus[1] projects have filled in parts of the research void on the use of VCI equipment in multilingual legal settings. Although these projects and other research cover many different grounds, the interpreter's perception of her role[2] remains largely unexplored.

This paper builds on the current body of knowledge in Interpreting Studies (IS) by examining eighteen interviews carried out with practising spoken language court interpreters in England and Wales. Their interviews are analysed through the medium of role-space, a relatively new theoretical framework developed by Llewellyn-Jones & Lee (2014).

The first two sections briefly review the literature on the use of VCI equipment in court and the interpreter's role, §3 summarises the methodology used, and §4 analyses the data gathered. Finally, §5 discusses the data in light of the findings from the literature review and formulates recommendations for interpreter training. It is posited that the use of technology enhances and/or creates different factors that can affect various aspects of the interpreter's role-space.

2 Videoconference interpreting in court settings

The use of VCI equipment in a legal setting was examined as early as the 1990s. Research at the time was mainly restricted to monolingual court settings, with a specific focus on the US court context (Radburn-Remfry 1994; Thaxton 1993). From then onwards, research in a monolingual setting has evolved mainly around three intrinsically related areas. First, scholars such as Johnson & Wiggins (2006) question the legality of using VCI technology to mediate a court hearing as it could

---

[1]Avidicus stands for Assessment of Videoconference Interpreting in the Criminal Justice Service.

[2]For purely stylistic reasons, the term 'interpreter' will sometimes be replaced by the feminine personal or possessive pronouns 'she' or 'her', whereas he/his/him will refer to either the defendant or the witness.

infringe the defendant's right to due process. Similarly, Radburn-Remfry (1994) and Thaxton (1993) raise concerns as regards the impact that VCI equipment could have on the fairness of the court proceedings. The second main research theme focuses on the impact that VCI equipment has on participants' perceptions of the court hearing, and how court participants interact. Studies reveal that it is more difficult to assess emotions (Radburn-Remfry 1994), body language (Fullwood et al. 2008), and a witness's credibility (Roth 2000). There is also a risk that participants feel detached from the process (McKay 2016), and the working relationship between the remote defendant and the participants in court may be questioned (Hodges 2008). Verdier & Licoppe (2011) also demonstrate that the conversation can be more fragmented, utterances can overlap (Licoppe 2015), and the defendant may be more reluctant to interact (Licoppe 2014). Finally, a number of studies have discussed technological issues, including the impact on interaction of poor sound and video quality (Haas 2006; Plotnikoff & Woolfson 2000). Another research area also seems to emerge as studies such as Licoppe et al. (2013) no longer investigate quality-related issues in terms of equipment, but they examine how the interaction itself is produced (e.g.: who orchestrates the camera moves, and how this affects the interaction).

In multilingual settings, studies on the use of VCI equipment form part of a relatively new research area, which has been primarily examined within the realm of the Avidicus projects. This research investigates the use of VCI and Remote Interpreting (RI) in various legal settings such as criminal courtrooms and police stations across Europe. They also offer training guidelines and recommendations to various legal stakeholders. Their studies are quite far reaching, and some of their findings confirm those in a monolingual setting. For instance, Avidicus 1 reveals that it is more difficult to establish a rapport with the participants on the other side of the screen (Rombouts 2011). It also demonstrates that VCI requires more synchronisation in terms of interaction and turn-taking, and it is more conducive to overlapping turns and artificial pauses (Balogh & Hertog 2011). Furthermore, interpreters reported that they found it more stressful, isolating, and tiring (Miler-Cassino & Rybińska 2011). In a bid to further explore the impact of VCI in a legal setting, Avidicus 2 establishes a list of interrelated factors that affect interpreting quality and a list of strategies developed by interpreters. It also offers some strategies to interpreters to overcome issues relating to the use of VCI. Finally, Avidicus 3 takes stock of the use of VCI equipment in twelve European countries and, for each of them, the findings are thematised under nine areas: procurement, equipment and maintenance, uses, participant distribution, pre-VC/post-VC, mode of interpreting, VCI management communication management, and working arrangements. According to Braun (2016), it transpires that in

England and Wales there are various VCI equipment suppliers operating, and VCI equipment is fitted within existing courtrooms, which can dictate the position of the screen and cameras. These set-ups can lead to various potential layouts and create different constraints. Furthermore, VCI hearings tend to be rather short, and are characterised by a lack of pre-briefing and debriefing sessions. Finally, the interpreter works mainly in consecutive mode, and the issue of rapport building with remote participants are further highlighted.

Other studies have been conducted in the area of VCI-mediated legal interpreting outside the realm of the Avidicus projects. For instance, Ellis (2004) examines the fairness of its use in refugee hearings in Canada. This report confirms that the use of VCI leads to a more impersonal means of communication, and it also highlights technical issues regarding poor audio and video quality. Similar conclusions are reported in the Bail for Immigration Detainees and the British Refugee Bail for Immigration Detainees and the British Refugee Council's (2008), and it also reveals that the use of VCI equipment distorts body language in immigration hearings. Furthermore, in English criminal courts, Fowler (2012) examines the use of equipment, the interpreter's working conditions, and the interaction management. Her studies show that the interpreter is a more visible court actor when VCI equipment is used. Finally, in a recent study Devaux (2017a), I investigated the interpreter's ethical rationalisation process and argued that interpreters rationalise ethical dilemmas mainly through their codes of ethics. However, specific ethical issues arise in VCI A and/or VCI B, for which other ethical paradigms, such as consequentialism or virtue ethics, need to be considered.

Overall, research carried out in VCI tends to focus on various paradigms that evolve around the use of VCI equipment and its impact on the interaction. Results show that there are similar difficulties in a mono- or multilingual context, be it related to technical difficulties or interaction management. Interestingly, the legality concerning the use of VCI is not as prominent a research area as it is in monolingual settings. Based on the literature review, it is also striking that the court interpreter's role in VCI is an underexplored research area, especially as this theme has been studied widely in various face-to-face contexts.

3 The court interpreter's role

The interpreter's role has been examined in many different public service settings, which has led to many role labels being coined. To name but a few, interpreters have been referred to as a conduit, a clarifier, a culture broker or an advocate (Niska 2002); a filter, a detective, a multi-purpose bridge, a diamond connoisseur, or a miner (Angelelli 2004); and a helper, a social worker, an advisor or an advocate (Grbic 2001).

Building on the seminal work by Wadensjö (1998), the body of research demonstrates that the interpreter can adopt different role labels during the same Interpreter-Mediated Event (IME). During psychotherapeutic sessions, Bot (2009) for instance, describes the role of the interpreter as a continuum where the interpreter as a conduit and the interpreter as an active participant are situated at either end of such a continuum. Similarly, Mason (2009) argues that the interpreter is an active member in immigration interviews, and her positionings will change and adapt in light of other participants' responses.

When examining the role of the court interpreter more specifically, the literature reveals that, contrary to the ideology often imposed by the court, the interpreter is a conduit (Laster & Taylor 1994), and she can also adopt several roles during a court hearing (Berk-Seligson 1990; Martin & Ortega Herráez 2009). Similar to other public service settings, many labels have been created to identify her role. For instance, Hale (2008) observes that the court interpreter can be: an advocate for the minority language speaker, an advocate for the institution of the service provider, a gatekeeper, a facilitator of communication, and a faithful renderer of the other's utterances. Other researchers describe the court interpreter's role as an impartial translation machine, a linguistic and cultural bridge, an expert witness (Mikkelson 1998), a cultural or linguistic mediator, or a communication facilitator (Nartowska 2016).

The above studies rely on attributing a role label with certain characteristics to the role(s) that researchers observe or analyse. However, Gentile et al. (1996: 32) state that a "kaleidoscope of role (…) is not conducive to the creation of a professional identity", and one could question the extent to which creating different role labels with sometimes blurred characteristics can contribute to a professional identity. A potential means to circumvent the creation of more role labels may reside in the use of role-space, a rather new theoretical framework in Interpreting Studies that became more widely-known due to Llewellyn-Jones & Lee's (2014) publication. Role-space is based on the three-dimensional conceptualisation of the interpreter's role alongside three axes. First, the z-axis, Presentation of Self, refers to the interpreter herself, and how much or how little information she provides about herself during an IME. The x-axis, Participant Alignment, indicates whether she is siding more towards one party, or whether she remains neutral. Finally, the y-axis, Interaction Management, indicates the extent to which she manages the interaction between the parties. Figure 1 summarises the template that is used in this study. Worth noting is the fact that a role-space model is organic and that the interpreter's presentation of self, participant alignment, and interaction management may fluctuate alongside their respective axes in order to reflect changes within an IME.

In order to design the interpreter's role-space, Llewellyn-Jones & Lee (2011: 4–5; 2013: 62) draw a sample list of criteria used to assess the court interpreter's presentation of self, participant alignment, and interaction management, which are summarised in Table 1.

Table 1: Sample list of role-space criteria

Presentation of Self	Interaction Management	Participant Alignment
The interpreter…		
introduces herself/takes the oath or affirms	requests for clarification or repetition	addresses specific participants directly
refers to herself as "the interpreter"	manages turn-taking	provides feedback and back-channels
gives insights into her personal likes/dislikes	requests specific actions	explains some aspects of the interpreting process
answers direct questions	requests change in the environment	smiles when a participant makes a humorous contribution
divulges personal information about herself		reads body language/establishes eye-contact

As an example which could illustrate Table 1, Llewellyn-Jones & Lee (2014: 77–78) report on the role-space that they adopted whilst interpreting during a court hearing. Their presentation of self was low as they introduced themselves as the interpreters, and then they were sworn in, but they did not provide the other participants with any further information about themselves. Their interaction management was quite high as they could seek clarification, and they could ask for questions to be reframed. However, they were more reluctant to regulate the interaction between participants. Finally, their participant alignment was limited to ensuring participants' understanding of the proceedings. As a result, they aligned equally between the participants, but they felt that their alignment was very low. Their role-space model is represented in Figure 2.

5 Technologies and role-space

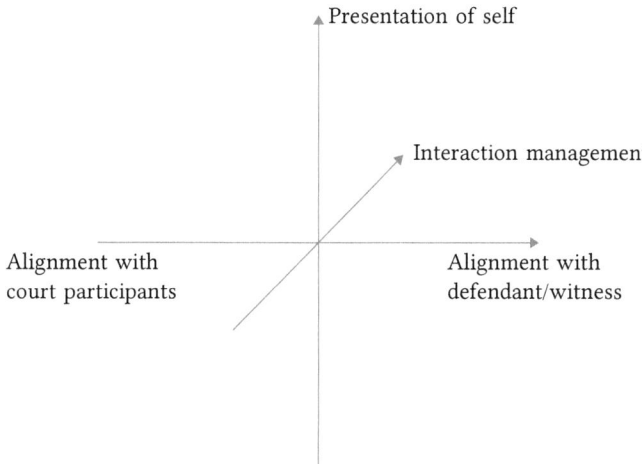

Figure 1: Llewellyn-Jones & Lee's (2014) role-space template

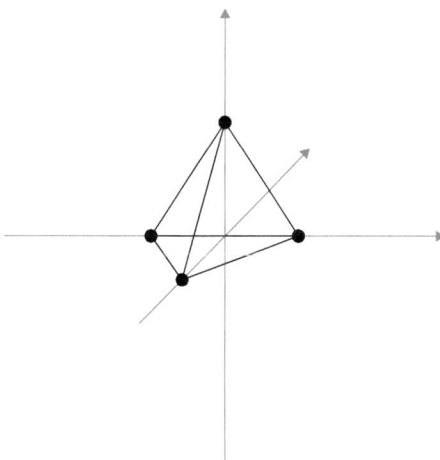

Figure 2: Llewellyn-Jones & Lee's (2014) role space model based on their court experience described above

4 Methodology and research design

From a methodological viewpoint, this study was anchored within Actor-Network Theory (ANT). Such an approach enables researchers to examine human and non-human actors as forming part of an interactive network.³ From an ANT ontological viewpoint, reality stems from the interplay created between human and non-human actors, and epistemologically, reality may be plural and unravelling it "requires identifying and following those actually involved in [the network's] creation" (Bonner 2013: 112). Applying ANT to this study enabled the researcher to examine how the interpreter, the other court participants, and the VCI equipment interacted, through the eyes of the interpreter, to create a network during the court hearing within which the interpreter would express her role-space.⁴

After obtaining ethical approval from the University of Salford to carry out the doctoral project, 1,150 prospective participants who were all members of the National Register of Public Service Interpreters (NRPSI) were contacted by email in 2014. Thirty-nine expressed an interest and, in the end, eighteen practising court interpreters in England and Wales were interviewed. When applying Seidman's (2006) principles of sufficiency and saturation of information, the number of participants was deemed sufficient.

In terms of participants' profiles, there were sixteen women and two men sharing, between them, a wide range of language combinations (mainly European languages, but also Arabic, Chinese, and Turkish). All participants had a Diploma in Public Service Interpreting (DPSI), or equivalent, which at the time was a requirement to become a court interpreter. Several participants had more than one qualification, and they often combined a DPSI with a degree or an MA in Languages or in Translation and Interpreting Studies. Most participants (twelve) had at least ten years' experience in court interpreting. Their experience in interpreting in VCI was somehow more limited with most participants having interpreted on 10 or fewer occasions in VCI A and/or B.

In line with the ANT's methodological stance, semi-structured interviews were conducted with the eighteen participants. The interview pointers were based on Table 1 in order to ensure that enough information was collected so that a role-space model could be drawn for each participant. The interviews were conducted either face-to-face or via Skype.⁵ The recordings were then transcribed verbatim

---

³For more information on ANT, Latour (2005) offers a good introduction on the interaction and networks created between humans and non-human entities.

⁴For more information on the extent to which ANT and role-space are compatible, see Devaux (2017b).

⁵For a more in-depth discussion on conducting interviews face-to-face or via Skype, see Devaux (2017b).

and coded using NVivo. The corpus gathered accounted for 12.5 hours of recording.

5 Data analysis through role-space

The eighteen participants taking part in this study expressed different role perceptions, and the results are summarised in Tables 2, 3, 4, and 5.

Table 2: Role-space in VCI A

	Presentation of self	Participant Alignment[a]	Interaction Management
P1	Very low	> Court	Very low
P3	Low	> Court	Low
P5	Low	Equal	High
P6	Low	Equal	Quite high
P7	Low	> Court	Low
P8	Very low	> Court	From low to high
P9	Low	> Court	High
P14	Low	Equal	From low to high
P15	Low	Equal	From very low to high
P16	Low	> Court	From low to quite high
P17	Low	> Court	Low
P18	Low	> Court	Low to quite high

[a]The sign ">" designates the side towards which the interpreter aligned.

The reasons explaining this assessment are summarised below. However, as some participants' models differed greatly from those presented in Table 2 and Table 3, their models are discussed separately in §5.4. Due to word constraints and in light of the various role-spaces created, this section offers a brief summary of the data analysis, and a more in-depth analysis is provided in Devaux (2017b).

5.1 Presentation of self

In VCI A, P1 and P8 could not introduce themselves and/or were not sworn-in when all parties were in attendance. P1 stated that she could have been "the cleaner, (…) the woman with the microphone." Similarly, P8 believed that it was not obvious to the defendant that she was the interpreter. P1 added that she

Table 3: Role-space in VCI B

	Presentation of self	Participant Alignment	Interaction Management
P1	Very low	Equal	Low
P2	Low	Equal	Low to quite high
P3	Low	> Defendant	High
P4	Low	> Witness	Quite high
P5	Low	Equal	High
P6	Low	Equal	Quite high
P11	Low	> Witness	High
P15	Low	Equal	Low to high
P16	Low	> Witness	Low to quite high
P18	Low	Equal	Low to quite high

believed it was difficult for interpreters to be perceived as impartial as the defendant was on the other side of the screen. Similarly, in VCI B, P1 stated the introduction/sworn-in process was missing. As such the presentation of self for these participants in these settings was deemed very low.

The other participants reported that they had been sworn-in. They had introduced themselves, as the interpreter, to all the parties on both sides of the screen. Most also believed that impartiality was not impaired by the use of VCI equipment. However, they did not divulge any further information, for instance about themselves. As such, their presentation of self was deemed low.

5.2 Participant alignment

Four participants in VCI A and six in VCI B reported that they were able to align equally between the participants on both sides of the screen. Although some reported that their ability to hear/see well may be slightly affected by the use of VCI equipment, it had never been so poor that it had affected their interpreting performance. In fact, one participant (P15) even reported that it was easier to see/hear the court participants in VCI A than when interpreting face-to-face from the dock. The participants were also able to replicate body language, give feedback, and intervene to explain cultural references, when needed.

The other participants' experience differed greatly. In VCI A, they reported that they encountered technical difficulties that impacted on their ability to hear and/or see the remote party well. They often stated that the sound was echoing, and P1 even compared the setting to a mausoleum. Furthermore, they felt that they could not read the witness or defendant's body language to obtain feedback or backchannel. Some also stated that the use of vci equipment had a negative impact on the proceedings as they could not interpret all the content, cultural references, and/or build a rapport with the defendant in vci a in order to adapt their terminology. Interestingly, the reason P9 aligned more towards the participants in court differs. She did not report on her inability to align with the defendant, but by sitting next to the judge, the close physical proximity made her over-align towards the participants in court. In vci b, participants stated that it was more difficult to replicate body language as the screens were too small. They also reported that although it was easier to build a relationship with the defendant/witness, it was more difficult to reproduce this with the participants in court. As a result, these participants aligned more towards the party with whom they were physically present.

5.3 Interaction management

Some participants perceived that their interaction management had been either very low, low, quite high, or high. Their reasons differed and are summarised below.

P1 felt that her interaction management was very low in vci a. She argued that the defendant was so removed from the process that no interaction could take place. Other participants' interaction management was low as they felt that the working environment was more daunting, and they were reluctant to interrupt the proceedings to ask for clarification. They also felt that the use of technology made the defendant less likely to interrupt the proceedings. On the other hand, some participants' interaction management was high or very high, be it in vci a or vci b. For instance, P6 and P9 said that it was easier to ask for repetitions and clarification as they were in clear view of the judge in vci a. P9 also said that she always mentioned to the defendant that he could interrupt her at any time, if he did not understand. On several occasions, the defendant then interrupted her in vci a, and she was able to manage the flow of interaction. Similarly, P4's interaction management in vci b was quite high. Although she did not encounter any instances of overlapping turns, she managed the interaction by asking the court to speak in "smaller chunks" as technology was used. Interestingly, she also stated that the defendant was less engaged in the proceedings, despite the interpreter being present in the same room. P5 managed the interaction by telling the defendant "Please don't talk, I am listening", and then she informed the court that the defendant had a question. In the same vein as P4's approach, P5 required the court to speak one sentence at a time.

The above participants' interaction management could be described as static in the sense that they perceived it to be either very low, low, quite high, or high in VCI A/B. Other participants perceived that their interaction management could be expressed alongside a continuum ranging from very low to high. These participants felt that there was no need/hardly any need to intervene during the VCI court hearing, be it in VCI A and/or VCI B. Hence, their interaction management was very low/low. Nonetheless, had the need occurred, they stated that it would be possible to have a quite high/high interaction management, and that the use of VCI technology would not impair their abilities to manage the interaction. The reasons put forward by the participants as to why interaction management in VCI was very low/low differed, and they can be summarised as follows:

1. the hearings tend to be quite short, hence reducing the opportunity to encounter cultural references

2. interpreter's expectation that the defendant would show enough respect to the court not to intervene

3. over-lapping turns tend to be more frequent at police stations

4. as the defendant appears remotely, he is less likely to intervene in court

5. the interventions were "quite clear and straightforward" (P15)

It would not be feasible to create a role-space model for each of the participants in this article.[6] However, the general shape of their models could be divided into two categories: those who perceived their interaction management as static, therefore creating a four-face-pyramid model (Figure 3), and those who perceived their interaction management as a continuum, thus forming a five-face-pyramid one (Figure 4).

5.4 Split role-space

Finally, some interpreters created one role-space for the participants in court and another one for defendant and witness. Their role-space axes are summarised in Tables 4 and 5.

The reasons justifying the above participants' alignment are similar to those mentioned previously. Therefore, they will not be analysed again, and this subsection will focus on their presentation of self and/or interaction management.

---

[6] A detailed role-space analysis for each participant and their role-space model is available in Devaux (2017b).

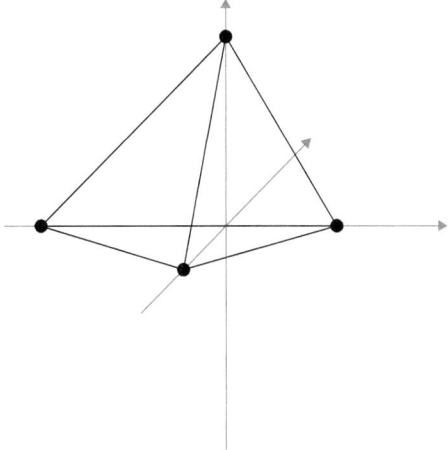

Figure 3: P9's four-shape model in VCI A

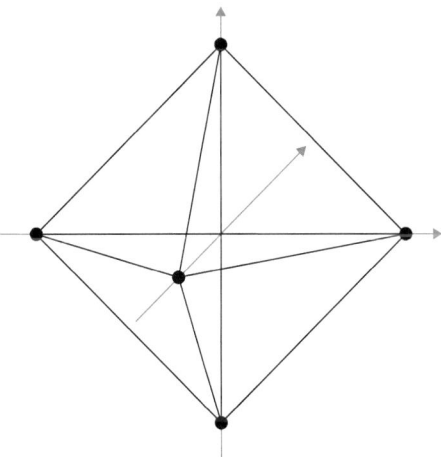

Figure 4: P15's five-face pyramid shape model in VCI A

Table 4: Split role-space in VCI A

	Presentation of self		Participant Alignment	Interaction management	
	Court	Defendant		Court	Defendant
P10	Low	Very low	> Court	High	Quite high
P12	Low	Very low	Equal	Low to quite high	

Table 5: Split role-space in VCI B

	Presentation of self		Participant Alignment	Interaction management	
	Court	Defendant		Court	Defendant
P13	Very low	Low	> Defendant and solicitor	Very low	Quite high
P14	Very low	Low	Equal	Low to quite high	
P17	Very low	Low	Equal	Low to high	

In VCI A and VCI B their presentation of self was low with the co-located party, and very low with the remote participant(s). They could introduce themselves as the court interpreter with their co-located party. However, they could not replicate the process with the remote party, or even be sworn-in, for instance. Also, P12 raised some concerns on how she could be perceived as impartial by the defendant in VCI A as she was seen "on the same side" of the court, and P13 thought it was more difficult to establish an atmosphere of trust with the participants in court in VCI B. Hence, their presentation was low with the co-located party and very low with the remote participant(s).

P12 in VCI A, and P14 and P17 in VCI B perceived their interaction management alongside a continuum ranging from low to quite high/high. Again, the reasons were similar to those for the participants above, so they will not be discussed here.

The interaction management for P10 in VCI A and P13 in VCI B differed between the participants in court and the remote defendant/witness. P10 believed that the use of VCI equipment did not impact on his ability to manage the interaction with the participants in court. Yet, P10's interaction management with the other side was lower as "giving the conversation a rhythm [had been] much more difficult" (P10) with the defendant. Similarly, P13's interaction management was very low with the participants in court. Although he had encountered difficulties hearing parts of the court interventions, he did not intervene to notify the participants

5 Technologies and role-space

in court of the issue. Nevertheless, his interaction management with the solicitor and the defendant was quite high as they were sitting together, and he could attract their attention, and ask them for repetitions/clarification.

As a result, these participants' role-space model was split, and their shapes differed greatly from the other participants, as illustrated by Figures 5 (P10), 6 (P12), 7 (P13), 8 (P14), and 9 (P17). Worth noting is that P12 in VCI A and P14 and P15 in VCI B created two 3D role-space models. In order to preserve their model's readability, it was decided to split them into two graphs: one representing her role-space model with the participants in court (on the left hand-side), and one with the defendant (on the right-hand side).

The participants perceived their role differently in VCI A and/or B, and, in fact, very few participants shared the exact same role-space (except, for instance, P3 and P7 in VCI A, and P12 in VCI A and P14 in VCI B). Although there were many different perceptions, their role-space can be grouped into three main categories: a fixed, a continuum, or a split role-space. Also, the use of equipment affected the participants' axes to various extents, and the distance between the participants meant that some interpreters were not always able to present themselves, manage aspects of the interaction, and/or align equally between the court participants. Worth noting is the fact that some participants mentioned that such equipment could also improve parts of the court proceedings. Notably, it was easier for some interpreters to seek clarification in VCI A.

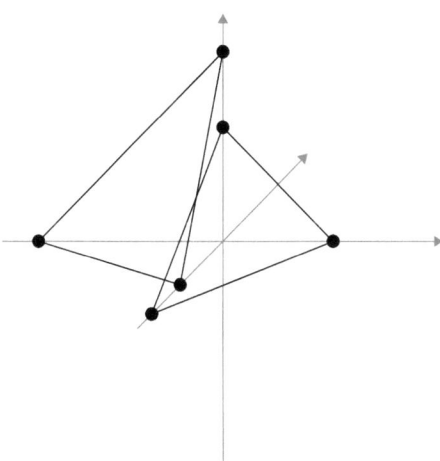

Figure 5: P10's role-space model in VCI A

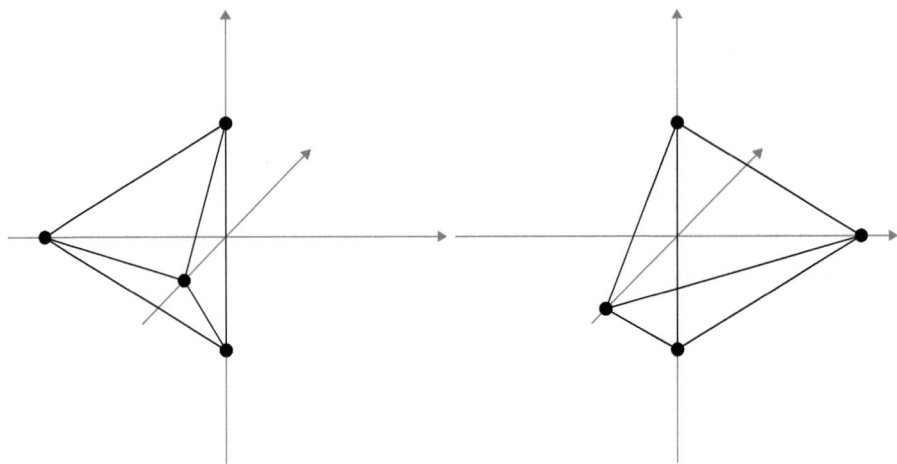

Figure 6: P12's role-space model with the court (left) and the defendant (right) in VCI A

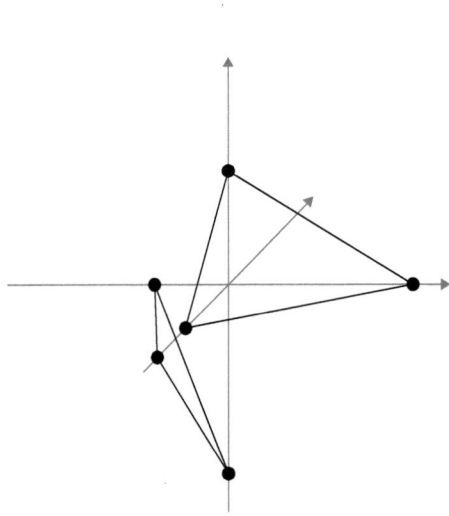

Figure 7: P13's role-space model in VCI B

5   *Technologies and role-space*

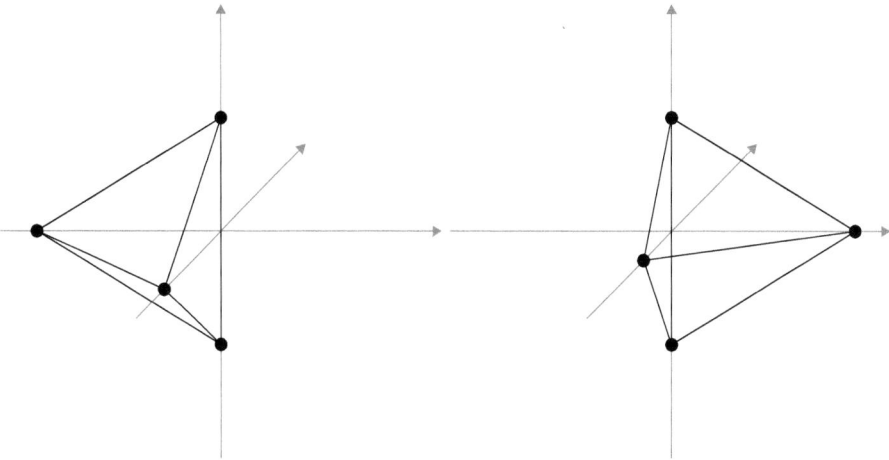

Figure 8: P14's role-space with the participants in court (left) and the witness (right) in VCI B

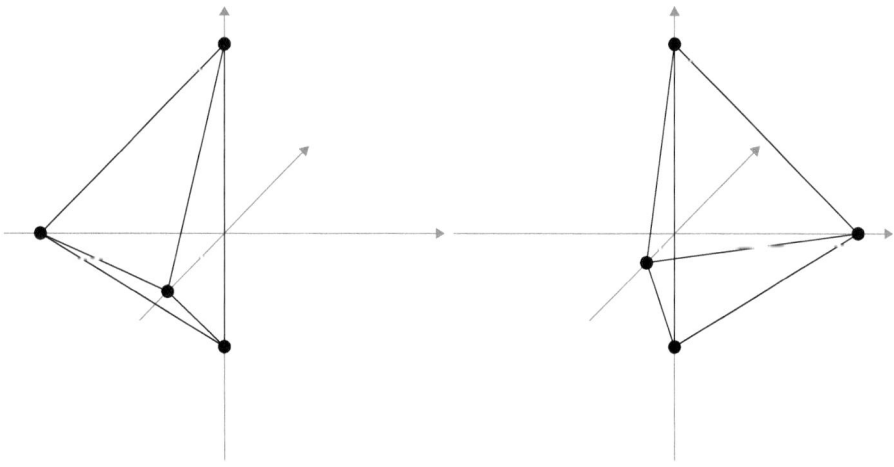

Figure 9: P17's role-space model with the participants in court (left) and the defendant (right) in VCI B

6 Discussion of findings

Building on the above findings, this section discusses the participants' perceptions of their role in light of the literature review, and it suggests some recommendations for training.

6.1 True-to-life experience

van Rotterdam & van den Hoogen (2011) argue that the use of vci equipment cannot represent a true-to-life experience due to various factors affecting the proceedings (such as potential poor quality of sound/picture, establishing eye contact, participants' reactions/interactions, etc.). In this study, parts of the data confirm that the absence of body language and back channelling, for instance, were highlighted as factors affecting some participants' experience, and these findings align with other studies which analyse the impact of the use of technologies. For instance, Radburn-Remfry (1994) argues that, in a mono-lingual setting, participants in court may feel more emotionally detached from the defendant during vci hearings. Hodges (2008) raises questions regarding the working relations between the defendant and the defence counsel. Supporting their studies, P1 felt that the defendant had not been taking part in his own hearing as he was too divorced from the proceedings. P1 believed that at this point, the right to see due legal process taking place could be questioned. This would support the idea that vci cannot replicate a true-to-life experience. It is worth noting that the participants' experience was not homogeneous, and it was even contradictory in some parts. For instance, P9 believed that when the defendant did not speak with a strong regional accent, there were no differences regarding whether the hearing was conducted in face-to-face or vci A mode. This plurality of interpreters' perceptions reflects this study's epistemological stance and the interpreters' multivocality. The array of perceptions is a window opening onto the actors' various realities, which suggests that a true-to-life experience can be a rather subjective notion, and from the interpreters' viewpoints vci equipment can impair or improve aspects of vc-conducted court hearing.

6.2 Factors affecting the interpreter's perception of her role

The interpreters' different role perceptions in this study are not a new phenomenon. Some studies in is offer several factors justifying the interpreters' perceptions of their role differently in face-to-face settings, such as qualifications (Martin & Abril Martí 2008) and cultural acceptability (Merlini 2009). One could also question the extent to which professional experience shape the interpreters' perceptions. All the participants in this study were DPSI qualified – some passed the same type of DPSI (e.g. law), and some were trained in the same centres. Yet, their role-spaces were different. Furthermore, some participants shared the same culture, but their role-space models differed. Finally, P1 and P2 in VCI B have many years of experience as court interpreters (20 and 15 years, respectively), but their role-spaces also differ. Similarly, P6 and P10 have both interpreted over ten times in VCI, but the role-spaces created are different. This tends to suggest that if qualification, cultural acceptability, and professional experience influence the participants' role perception in this study, these could only be factors partly contributing to shaping such perceptions. Nevertheless, the recurring denominator when analysing the interviews seems to be the extent to which the participants felt that the use of VCI equipment had limited parts of their role-space.

Due to the use of VCI equipment, some participants had a very low presentation of self as they could not introduce themselves and/or be sworn-in. In her study, Fowler (2013) observed that some interpreters were not introduced at the start of the hearing. In such instances, there was "a tendency for the interpreter to defer to the court in matters which were properly part of their own professional remit" (Fowler 2013: 245). P1 raised the sitting arrangement as a potential issue with being perceived as impartial. This has been identified as a potential issue in the Avidicus 2's research report, where their findings show that "the seating arrangements gave the impression that the participants on one side of the video link spoke 'as one' or 'could be perceived as one'" (Braun 2013: 53). However, it is worth noting that other participants perceived that the seating arrangement was in fact improving aspects of their role-space as they were no longer interpreting from the dock at the back of the courtroom.

Some participants also aligned more towards one party as they felt that the technical difficulties encountered, and/or the lack of feedback or back-channelling opportunities, had not enabled them to establish a rapport with the court participant(s) on the other side of the screen. As a result, their participant alignment with the remote party had been lower. These findings align with Rombouts's (2011) and Napier's (2011) studies, which reveal that it is more difficult to establish a rapport with the remote party, or with Braun et al. (2016: 4), who asserts that VCI "entail[s] a reduction in the quality of the intersubjective relations between the participants." This study also shows that when the interpreters' participant alignment differs between actors, there had been a greater tendency to align towards the participants in court, rather than the witness or, to even a lesser extent, the defendant. Although the findings partly corroborate the difficulty to establish a rapport with the remote party, they also suggest that there are alignment disparities between the court actors and, amongst all the participants, the defendant is the party that the interpreter may be the least willing to over-align towards.

Finally, a few participants believed that the use of vci equipment had slightly reduced their interaction management, but overall it had remained quite high, which is similar to Llewellyn-Jones & Lee's (2014) experience as court interpreters. Other participants had a high interaction management, whilst others had perceived it as ranging from low to high. Only a few participants had felt that their interaction management had been low. To some extent, the data gathered in this study concurs partially with the literature review, in the sense that court interpreters have to manage the interaction by giving turns, for instance (Angelelli 2003; Llewellyn-Jones & Lee 2014; Martin & Abril Martí 2008), and they have to do so even more when technologies are used, to the extent that they become fully-fledged independent actors (Lee 2007; Rosenberg 2007). Similarly, Braun (2016) argues that the discourse is more fragmented in vci-conducted legal proceedings, and it is therefore not surprising that many participants had a quite high or high interaction management. What remains unclear, though, is the reason why some court interpreters failed to intervene in order to re-balance their interaction management.

The use of vci equipment affected the participants' axes to varying degrees and very few participants' role-space was similar to Llewellyn-Jones & Lee's (2014) court experience (Figure 2). Despite such differences the shapes of most participants' role-space models were similar to the types discussed in Llewellyn-Jones & Lee's (2014) work. Indeed, some interpreters perceived their role as a 3D fixed entity, whilst other created a 3D continuum. However, unlike Llewellyn-Jones & Lee's (2014) models in face-to-face settings, this study reveals that the interpreter can adopt a third type of model, whereby she splits her role-space into two sub-spaces. In these instances, this study's participants felt that the use of technology had a limited impact on their role perceptions with their co-located party, but it restricted aspects of their role-space with the remote party.

6.3 Recommendations for training

As mentioned by some participants and as confirmed when examining the IoL Educational Trust's (2015) *Handbook for Candidates* sitting the dpsi examination, it seems that vci training does not form an integral part of the dpsi curriculum. Therefore, given the fact that vci is used in court, and given the impact that the equipment can have on the interpreter's perception of her role, it is recommended that training in the use of VCI in court be offered.

In order to ensure that prospective court interpreters possess more than a conceptual understanding of VCI, DPSI centres should give students the opportunity to observe proceedings taking place in both VCI A and B modes. It is also important that trainees are given the opportunity to practise role-plays in these two modes. Although centres may not be equipped with VCI technologies meeting the International Telecommunication Union's (2009) H323 Recommendation, trainees could nonetheless practise role-plays using cruder technologies such as Skype. Furthermore, the aim of this article was not to develop or assess a curriculum for trainee PSIs. However, centres could usefully develop resources based on the Braun et al. (2011) or Avidicus 3 training outline.

Participants also reported that court actors sometimes lack etiquette in terms of VCI equipment and its use, making it more difficult for the interpreter to hear the proceedings. For instance, court staff or members of the public would leave the courtroom mid-hearing, court members would rustle papers near their microphone, or they would not speak in their microphone. Therefore, it is essential that legal practitioners also receive training in using VCI equipment. Such training would need to make specific reference to conducting a bilingual VCI hearing in the presence of an interpreter. As mentioned by some interpreters, training should not take place independently from the other participants, but rather all the court participants should also jointly train in using VCI equipment. This confirms the recommendations put forward by other scholars such as Braun (2011) and Fowler (2012).

It is worth noting that such training may also be relevant to practising court interpreters. The NRPSI has more than 2,000 registrants who are dispersed over a large geographical zone. A means to ensure that they are trained in VCI mode could be for the NRPSI to offer CPD sessions to its members on this interpreting mode.

7 Conclusions

This article reported on the findings arising from Devaux's (2017b) doctoral thesis. Based on the analysis of eighteen interviews conducted with court interpreters in England and Wales, it emerged that the interpreters perceived their role differently in VCI, and they created different role-space models. The use of VCI equipment affected various aspects of their presentation of self, participant alignment, and/or interaction management. Given the increasing use of VCI equipment in court, this article also made some recommendations for training court interpreters. Although this study includes some limitations (e.g. a limited number of participants, who were all DPSI qualified), it paves the way to avenues for further research. To give a more generic picture of the court interpreter's role, this study's findings could be complemented by recruiting court interpreters without a DPSI (or equivalent). Another avenue to complement this study would be to observe court interpreters' role when VCI is used, and to interview the other court participants so that the impact of the interpreter's role in VCI could be examined. Furthermore, role-space is a relatively new theoretical framework and, as such, it would benefit from further empirical studies across various settings. Finally, it emerges from this study that some interpreters created a split-role model. The effect that this new model may have on the court participants and on the overall interaction is unknown and it would deserve further exploration.

References

Angelelli, Claudia. 2003. The interpersonal role of the interpreter in cross-cultural communication: A survey of conference, court and medical interpreters in the US, Canada, Mexico. In Louise Brunette, Georges L. Bastin, Isabelle Hemlin & Heather Clarke (eds.), *The critical link 3: Interpreters in the community*, 15–26. Amsterdam/Philadelphia: John Benjamins.

Angelelli, Claudia. 2004. *Medical interpreting and cross-cultural communication*. Cambridge: Cambridge University Press.

Bail for Immigration Detainees and the British Refugee Council. 2008. *A monitoring exercise by bail for immigration detainees and the refugee council: Immigration bail hearings by video link*. http://www.refugeecouncil.org.uk/assets/0001/7078/RC_and_BID_report_on_Bail_hearings_and_video_links_Mar_08, accessed 2012-4-15.

Balogh, Katalin & Eric Hertog. 2011. AVIDICUS comparative studies - part II: Traditional, video-conference and remote intepreting in police interviews. In Sabine Braun & Judith L. Taylor (eds.), *Videoconference and remote interpreting in criminal proceedings (pp.* 101–116. Guildford: University of Surrey.

Berk-Seligson, Susan. 1990. *The bilingual courtroom: Court interpreters in the judicial process*. Chicago/London: University of Chicago Press.

Bonner, William. 2013. History and IS: Broadening our view and understanding: Actor-network theory as a methodology. *Journal of Information Technology* 28(2). 111–123.

Bot, Hanneke. 2009. Role models in mental health interpreting. In Raquel de Pedro Ricoy, Isabelle Anne Perez & Christine Wilson (eds.), *Interpreting and translating in public service settings – policy, practice, pedagogy*, 115–126. Manchester: St Jerome.

Braun, Sabine. 2011. Recommendations for the use of video-mediated interpreting in criminal proceedings. In Sabine Braun & Judith L. Taylor (eds.), *Videoconference and remote interpreting in criminal proceedings*, 265–287. Guildford: University of Surrey.

Braun, Sabine. 2013. *AVIDICUS 2 – Action 2 research report: Assessment of video-mediated interpreting in the criminal justice system*. https://www.academia.edu/19593187/2013_AVIDICUS_2_final_research_report, accessed 2016-11-25.

Braun, Sabine. 2016. The European AVIDICUS projects: Collaborating to assess the viability of video-mediated interpreting in legal proceedings. *European Journal of Applied Linguistics* 4(1). 173–180.

Braun, Sabine, Elena Davitti & Sara Dicerto. 2016. *The use of videoconferencing in proceedings conducted with the assistance of an interpreter*. http://www.videoconference-interpreting.net/wp-content/uploads/2016/11/AVIDICUS3_Research_Report.pdf, accessed 2016-11-18.

Braun, Sabine, Judith L. Taylor, Joanna Miler-Cassino, Zofia Rybińska, Katalin Balogh, Eric Hertog & Dirk Rombouts. 2011. Training in video-mediated interpreting in legal proceedings: Modules for interpreting students, legal interpreters and legal practitioners. In Sabine Braun & Judith L. Taylor (eds.), *Videoconference and remote interpreting in criminal proceedings*, 233–288. Guildford: University of Surrey.

Devaux, Jérôme. 2017a. Virtual presence, ethics and videoconference interpreting: Insights from court settings. In Carmen Valero Garcés & Rebecca Tipton (eds.), *Ideology, ethics and policy development in public service interpreting and translation*, 131–150. Bristol: Multilingual Matters.

Devaux, Jérôme. 2017b. *Technologies in interpreter-mediated criminal court hearings an actor-network theory account of the interpreter's perception of her role-space*. Salford: University of Salford dissertation. https://open.academia.edu/JeromeDevaux, accessed 2018-5-1.

Ellis, Ronald. 2004. *Videoconferencing in refugee hearings*. http://www.irb-cisr.gc.ca/Eng/transp/ReviewEval/Pages/Video.aspx#author, accessed 2016-12-17.

Fowler, Yvonne. 2012. *Non-English-speaking defendants in the magistrates' court*. Birmingham: Aston University dissertation. http://eprints.aston.ac.uk/19442/1/Studentthesis-2013.pdf.

Fowler, Yvonne. 2013. Business as usual? Prison video link in the multilingual courtroom. In Christina Schäffner, Krzysztof Kredens & Yvonne Fowler (eds.), *Interpreting in a changing landscape: Selected papers from critical link 6*, 226–248. Amsterdam/Philadelphia: John Benjamins.

Fullwood, Chris, Amy Judd & Mandy Finn. 2008. *The effect of initial meeting context and video-mediation on jury perceptions of an eyewitness.* http://www.internetjournalofcriminology.com/Fullwood,%5C%20Judd%5C%20&%5C%20Finn%5C%20-%5C%20Video%5C%20Mediation.pdf, accessed 2012-8-1.

Gentile, Adolfo, Uldis Ozolins & Mary Vasilakos. 1996. *Liaison interpreting: A handbook.* Melbourne: Melbourne University Press.

Grbic, Nadja. 2001. First steps on firmer ground: A project for the further training of sign language interpreters in Austria. In Ian Mason (ed.), *Triadic exchanges: Studies in dialogue interpreting*, 149–171. Manchester: St Jerome.

Haas, Aaron. 2006. Videoconferencing in immigration proceedings. *Pierce Law Review* 5(1). 59–90.

Hale, Sandra. 2008. Controversies over the role of the court interpreter. In Carmen Valero Garcés & Anne Martin (eds.), *Crossing borders in community interpreting – definitions and dilemmas*, 203–230. Amsterdam/Philadelphia: John Benjamins.

Hodges, Louise. 2008. *Towards a European e-justice strategy.* Retrieved on 25 November 2014 from http://www.ecba.org/content/index.php?option=com_content&view=article&id=533upcoming-edinburgh-scotland-spring-conference-sp-1153635615&catid=88&Itemid=127.

International Telecommunication Union. 2009. *Series h: Audiovisual and multimedia systems - Infrastructure of audiovisual services.* https://www.itu.int/rec/T-REC-H.323-200912-I/en, accessed 2016-10-18.

IoL Educational Trust. 2015. *Diploma in public service interpreting: Handbook for candidates.* https://www.ciol.org.uk/sites/default/files/Handbook-DPSI.pdf, accessed 2018-11-21.

Johnson, Molly & Elizabeth Wiggins. 2006. Videoconferencing in criminal proceedings: Legal and empirical issues and directions for research. *Law & Policy* 28(2). 211–227.

Laster, Kathy & Veronica Taylor. 1994. *Interpreters and the legal system.* Sydney: The Federation Press.

Latour, Bruno. 2005. *Reassembling the social: An introduction to actor-network theory.* Oxford: Oxford University Press.

Lee, Jieun. 2007. Telephone interpreting: Seen from the interpreters' perspective. *Interpreting* 9(2). 231–252.

Licoppe, Christian. 2014. Two modes of referring to the case file in the courtroom: The use of indirect reported text and text-as-addressed speech in case summaries. *Language and Communication* 36. 83–96.

Licoppe, Christian. 2015. Video communication and "camera actions": The production of wide video shots in courtrooms with remote defendants. *Journal of Pragmatics* 76. 117–134.

Licoppe, Christian, Maud Verdier & Laurence Dumoulin. 2013. Courtoom interaction as a multimedia event: The work of producing relevant videoconference frames in French pre-trial hearings. *The Electronic Journal of Communication* 23. http://www.cios.org/EJCPUBLIC/023/1/023125.HTML, accessed 2016-11-20.

Llewellyn-Jones, Peter & Robert Lee. 2011. *Re-visiting role: Arguing for a multi-dimensional analysis of interpreter behaviour.* http://clok.uclan.ac.uk/5031/1/Lee%20and%20L-J%202011.pdf, accessed 2016-12-19.

Llewellyn-Jones, Peter & Robert Lee. 2013. Getting to the core of role: Defining interpreters' role-space. *International Journal of Interpreter Education* 5(2). 54–72.

Llewellyn-Jones, Peter & Robert Lee. 2014. *Redefining the role of the community interpreter: The concept of role-space.* Carlton-le-Moorland, Lincoln, United Kingdom: SLI Press.

Martin, Anne & Isabel Abril Martí. 2008. Community interpreter self-perception: A spanish case study. In Valero-Garcés Carmen & Anne Martin (eds.), *Crossing borders in community interpreting: Definitions and dilemmas*, 203–230. Amsterdam/Philadelphia: John Benjamins.

Martin, Anne & Juan Miguel Ortega Herráez. 2009. Court interpreters' self perception: A spanish case study. In Raquel de Pedro Ricoy, Isabelle Anne Perez & Christine Wilson (eds.), *Interpreting and translating in public service settings: Policy, practice, pedagogy*, 141–155. Manchester: St Jerome.

Mason, Ian. 2009. Role, positioning and discourse in face-to-face interpreting. In Raquel de Pedro Ricoy, Isabelle Anne Perez & Christine Wilson (eds.), *Interpreting and translation in public service settings: Policy, practice, pedagogy*, 52–73. Manchester: St Jerome.

McKay, Carolyn. 2016. Video links from prison: Permeability and the carceral world. *International Journal for Crime, Justice and Social Democracy* 5(1). 21–37.

Merlini, Raffaela. 2009. Interpreters in emergency wards: An empirical study of doctor-interpreter-patient interaction. In Raquel de Pedro Ricoy, Isabelle Anne Perez & Christine Wilson (eds.), *Interpreting and translating in public service settings: Policy, practice, pedagogy*, 89–114. Manchester: St Jerome.

Mikkelson, Holly. 1998. Towards a redefinition of the role of the court interpreter. *Interpreting* 3(1). 21–45.

Miler-Cassino, Joanna & Zofia Rybińska. 2011. AVIDICUS comparative studies – part III: Traditional interpreting and videoconference interpreting in prosecution interviews. In Sabine Braun & Judith L. Taylor (eds.), *Videoconference and remote interpreting in criminal proceedings*, 117–136. Guildford: University of Surrey.

Napier, Jemina. 2011. Here or there? An assessment of video remote signed language interpreter-mediated interaction in court. In Sabine Braun & Judith L. Taylor (eds.), *Videoconference and remote interpreting in criminal proceedings*, 145–185. Guildford: University of Surrey.

Nartowska, Karolina. 2016. The role of the court interpreter: A powerless or powerful participant in criminal proceedings? *The Interpreters' Newsletter* 20. 9–32.

Niska, Helge. 2002. Community interpreting training: Past, present and future. In Maurizio Viezzi & Giuliana Garzone (eds.), *Interpreting in the 21st century: Challenges and opportunities*, 133–144. Amsterdam/Philadelphia: John Benjamins.

Plotnikoff, Joyce & Richard Woolfson. 1999. *Preliminary hearings: Video links evaluation of pilot projects.* http://lexiconlimited.co.uk/wp-content/uploads/2013/01/Videolink-magistrates.pdf, accessed 2016-11-12.

Plotnikoff, Joyce & Richard Woolfson. 2000. *Evaluation of video link pilot project at Manchester crown court: Final report.* http://lexiconlimited.co.uk/wp-content/uploads/2013/01/Videolink-Crown.pdf, accessed 2016-11-12.

Radburn-Remfry, Patricia. 1994. Due process concerns in video production of defendants. *Stetson Law Review* 23. 805–838.

Rombouts, Dirk. 2011. The police interview using videoconferencing with a legal interpreter: A critical view from the perspective of interview technique. In Sabine Braun & Judith L. Taylor (eds.), *Videoconference and remote interpreting in criminal proceedings*, 159–166. Guildford: University of Surrey.

Rosenberg, Brett Allen. 2007. A data-driven analysis of telephone interpreting. In Cecilia Wadensjö, B. Englund Dimitrova & Nilsson Anna-Lena (eds.), *The critical link 4: Professionalisation of interpreting in the community*, 65–76. Amsterdam/Philadelphia: John Benjamins.

Roth, Michael. 2000. Laissez faire videoconferencing: Remote witness testimony and adversarial truth. *UCLA Law Review* 48(1). 185–220.

Seidman, Irving. 2006. *Interviewing as qualitative research: A guide for researchers in education and the social sciences.* 3rd edn. New York: Teachers College Press.

Thaxton, Ronnie. 1993. Injustice telecast: The illegal use of closed-circuit television arraignments and bail bond hearings in federal court. *Iowa Law review* 79(1). 175–202.

van Rotterdam, Peter & Ronald van den Hoogen. 2011. True-to-life requirements for using videoconferencing in legal proceedings. In Sabine Braun & Judith L. Taylor (eds.), *Videoconference and remote interpreting in criminal proceedings*, 187–198. Guildford: University of Surrey.

Verdier, Maud & Christian Licoppe. 2011. Videoconference in French courtrooms: Its consequences on judicial settings. *International Journal of Law, Language & Discourse* 1.3. 8–36.

Wadensjö, Cecilia. 1998. *Interpreting as interaction*. London: Longman.

Chapter 6

Present? Remote? Remotely present! New technological approaches to remote simultaneous conference interpreting

Klaus Ziegler
AIIC Technical Committee

Sebastiano Gigliobianco
SDI München

> Since the 1970s, there have been several approaches to test and implement remote interpreting as a complementary interpreting modality in addition to the traditional and proven interpretation on site. The reasons for experimenting with remote interpretation in conference settings are manifold and can generally be classified by economic aspects, availability issues or organizational matters. In this paper, we discuss the preliminary results of a pilot study aimed at exploring how the limitations of remote interpreting described by the literature could be overcome using new technological advances in Information and Communication Technology. We discuss challenges and technological solutions for remote simultaneous conference interpreting from an interdisciplinary perspective and sketch out what the future workspace for conference interpreters might look like.

1 Introduction

Since the 1970s, there have been several approaches to test and implement remote interpreting as a complementary interpreting modality in addition to the traditional and proven interpretation on site, with all the parties involved (speakers, audience and interpreters) being present in the same room, thus communicating in a more or less face-to-face scenario. The reasons for experimenting with remote interpretation in conference settings are manifold and can generally be classified by economic aspects (e.g. reduced travel costs for interpreters and/or speakers and/or audience), availability issues (e.g. no local interpreters available for a specific language combination) or organizational matters (e.g. an interpreter team can be hired within a shorter period of time, the room design does not allow for interpreting booths or booths are simply not wanted to be seen in the room).

Despite the encouraging results of studies, tests and experiments carried out throughout history, e.g. at UNESCO in 1976 (Kurz 2000), the United Nations in 1978 (Chernov 2004), in 1982 (UNESCO 1987), and in 2001 (Mouzourakis 2006), the European Union in 1992 (Kurz 2000), in 2001 (European Parliament Interpretation Directorate 2001) and 2005 (Roziner & Shlesinger 2010) using different technologies to transmit of audio and video signals from and to interpreters, there have always been two main factors preventing the large scale implementation of remote conference interpretation: technological limitations (due to insufficient availability of bandwidth for the synchronized transmission of sound and image with the necessary quality when transmitting via the Internet or telecommunication network, or very high costs when using satellite communication, either exclusively or along with terrestrial transmission technologies) and the more or less general refusal of the use of the so-called "new technologies" by conference interpreters. Apart from measurable physiological factors, like fatigue and stress leading to symptoms such as headaches and concentration problems, interpreters used to complain about the unease they were feeling because of not "being there" Mouzourakis (2006: 56), not having the possibility to get the right feel for the situation and not being able to interact directly with the other participants of the event. These psychological symptoms were mainly attributed to the limited view of the speaker and the audience.

In the last few years, general conditions for conference interpreting have been changing constantly not only due to globalization and altered market needs, but also due to digitalization and extremely fast developing information and communication technologies. The availability of hardware and software for dynamic monitoring and controlling of important parameters, such as lip synchronization, latency, video resolution and frequency response, as well as network infrastructures that allow for simultaneous transmission of high definition video and high quality audio signals via the Internet, combined with latest video, virtual reality and augmented reality (AR) technologies might offer possibilities to overcome existing technological, physiological and psychological problems.

2 Interdisciplinary and terminological challenges

One major challenge when discussing "remote interpreting" as a method for the delivery of interpreting services is the fact that there are a lot of different concepts being used in practice by the different stakeholders when referring to this method. We can observe that there is still no harmonized terminology being used even by technical experts and researchers. This linguistic phenomenon can be explained to a certain extent by the fact that interpreters, in general, are not experts in this technical field. Therefore, they tend to use technical concepts without knowing exactly what the technical background for certain scenarios is and what the implications of a certain technical setup are. Technically speaking, a video conference and video conferencing can be defined as

> a live, visual connection between two or more people residing in separate locations for the purpose of communication. At its simplest, video conferencing provides transmission of static images and text between two locations. At its most sophisticated, it provides transmission of full-motion video images and high-quality audio between multiple locations (TechTarget Network 2017).

This definition shows that the same concept is being used for a wide variety of technical setups.

When it comes to including interpreters to facilitate the necessary translation between the languages spoken by the participants in a communicative event, things become even more diffused. The term 'remote interpreting', one of the most widely used concepts, covers a whole range of technologically different setups. These setups range from a traditional presence-based scenario where interpreters, main speakers and the audience are concentrated at one event location, and one or several secondary speakers are connected from a distance for a limited duration, to a situation where none of the actors within the triad, speaker-listener-interpreter, are at the same location as the others.

Braun takes up this terminological challenge by saying that

> Two main uses of telephone and videoconference communication can be distinguished in connection with interpreting. One of these, remote interpreting (RI), refers to the use of communication technologies to gain access to an interpreter in another room, building, town, city or country. In this setting, a telephone line or videoconference link is used to connect the interpreter to the primary participants, who are together at one site. (Braun 2015: 1)

This definition excludes a setup where the participants are located at different locations. For this case, she introduces the concept of "teleconference interpreting to cover both telephone and videoconference communication" (Braun 2015: 2). Further on, she introduces as a separate term teleconference interpreting to cover both telephone and videoconference communication (ibid.)

For disambiguity purposes, she then introduces the terms "telephone-based interpreting" and "videoconference-based interpreting" (ibid.), but adds that there are a lot of additional concepts being used in practice.

For the purposes of this article, we broaden up the perspective and adhere to the definition given in the recently published ISO 20108:2016, introducing the term of "distance interpreting" (with "remote interpreting" as admitted term), giving the definition of "interpreting of a speaker in a different location from that of the interpreter, enabled by information and communications technology (ICT)".

Analyzing technological, communicative, cognitive, physiological and psychological aspects, it becomes clear very soon that every single dislocation of one of the emitting or receiving elements (speaker, listener or interpreter) to a different location (thus becoming a distant location) has a considerable impact on the technological setup and the components and transmission channels needed to enable communication between the different parties involved.

Furthermore, communicative aspects like verbal and non-verbal communication are altered by the rearrangement of the setting, as elements like gestures, facial expressions, cannot be perceived directly anymore, and have to be captured, transmitted and reproduced again at the distant site in order to be made available.

As for cognition, the cognitive load is also being influenced significantly by every alteration of the setting (Moser-Mercer 2005). Such a load is generated by additional, or at least altered, receptive and productive tasks related to the sub-processes of listening to a source text, processing its content and re-producing that content in the target language. Research has shown that cognition is intimately linked to physiological processes that take place in the human body, especially the brain as the controlling unit, and that a variation of acoustic and visual input to interpreters has an impact on vital functional systems such as the respiratory system and metabolism, leading to stress, early onset of fatigue and other phenomena (Moser-Mercer 2003).

Last but not least, there is also a wide range of psychological factors that have to be considered when approaching distance interpreting from an interdisciplinary point of view. In an ideal setting, communication taking place with all participants being at the same location, in the same room and with no obstacles impeding direct mutual perception, allows the participants in the communicative event to make use of at least four out of the five basic human senses: touch, smell, sight, hearing. Most of the related parameters, such as neuronal stimulation for haptic feedback, composition of ambient air for smelling, audio frequencies for hearing and light waves for vision can easily be measured, quantified and evaluated. However, other phenomena such as energy fields (sometimes referred to as mental, astral/emotional and etheric/physical bodies) that affect the balance of both the physical body and the non-physical mind are much more difficult to capture and evaluate, although they might have an influence on human interaction and, by that, on communication.

Whereas many interesting aspects related to distance interpreting have been addressed based on other interpreting specializations, such as legal interpreting (see AVIDICUS projects 1–3), there have not yet been similar large-scale projects directly or indirectly related to distance simultaneous conference interpreting. However, several aspects have been studied on a smaller scale, such as stress and performance in remote interpreting (Moser-Mercer 2003; Roziner & Shlesinger 2010), perception of remote interpreting by interpreters (Mouzourakis 2006) or visual input (Rennert 2008; Luisetto 2016).

3 Solutions in the past

3.1 Tests and experiments: UNESCO and the UN

Since the seventies, due to the rapid development in telecommunication technology, big international institutions, such as the United Nations and the European Union have begun testing new interpreting solutions to reduce the cost of conferences (UNESCO 1987: 26).

One of the first experiments with remote interpreting took place in 1976 when the UNESCO organized its General Assembly in Nairobi. The interpreters, however, were asked to work from Paris, which was connected to the capital city of Kenia through a satellite connection which provided an audio-video connection quality equal to that of a standard TV broadcast (Mouzourakis 1996: 30). The interpreters were not satisfied with their performance and stated that they were more tired and stressed than usual (Kurz 2000: 294).

A second experiment with remote interpreting was organized in 1978 by the United Nations. The conference was held in Buenos Aires and there were interpreters working both in Buenos Aires and in New York, the latter received audio-video signals through a satellite connection. The results showed that it was possible for the interpreters working in New York to achieve high quality interpretation (UNESCO 1987: 26), although the interpreters working in Buenos Aires were able to deliver a better performance due to their more intensive preparation and knowledge about the conference (Chernov 2004: 82–90).

Another experiment with satellite connection took place in Vienna in 1982 during the United Nations conference on the Exploration and Peaceful Use of Outer Space. At this conference, the interpreters worked in Vienna as well, but not in the same building (Andres & Falk 2009: 10). The communication was a success, but the interpreters complained about increased stress (UNESCO 1987: 26).

Although these experiments with satellite connection between the 70s and the 80s demonstrated that remote interpreting was possible, the huge costs and the increased level of stress led to the conclusion that this technology was too expensive and immature to be used yet (ibid. 26).

Thanks to the ongoing advancement of ICT and the growth of the European Union, new possibilities for remote interpreting arose. From the beginning of the 90s the European Union was the main driving force behind this development with the aim to create a central hub where the interpreters could work (Braun & Taylor 2011: 3).

One of the first positive results was achieved in 1999 in Vienna. ISDN technology was used during a UN Inter-Agency Meeting on Language Arrangements, Documentation and Publications, which was held in Geneva and interpreted from Vienna. During this experiment, the transmitted audio signals were based on a frequency going up to 7 kHz for the first time. The conference hall in Geneva was recorded by three cameras and the pictures were projected in Vienna using a projection screen with a transmission rate of 384 kbps (Mouzourakis 2006: 63). The audience was satisfied with the performance of the interpreters, and for the first time the interpreters were pleased with the quality of the audio transmission, although they criticized the video quality (Andres & Falk 2009: 11). Two months later, a second experiment was organized together with the International Telecommunication Union (ITU) and the École de Traduction et d'Interprétation (ETI). For this experiment, two French booths were installed: one in the conference hall and a second one in a remote location. In this case, the audio signal was encoded in MP3 format and the video signal was transmitted at a rate of 382 kbps (Mouzourakis 2006: 63). The audience received the signal from the local and remote booth alternately and was happy with the results. The interpreters, on the other hand, perceived the physical distance to the conference hall as negative and felt as if they were losing control over the situation. Interestingly, saliva samples were taken from both booths before and after the conference; contrary to what the interpreters stated, no relevant difference was noted in stress hormones (Moser-Mercer 2003).

A new experiment was conducted in 2001 in New York by the United Nations in which both ISDN and satellite connections were tested. The conference was recorded using three cameras and a 42- and 25-inch plasma screens were installed in front of the booths. With this experiment, the UN laid down the following minimum requirements for remote interpreting:

> 14 kHz sound (requiring 128 kbps) for sending floor sound to the booths (14 kHz) and 10 kHz sound (at 64 kbps) for sending interpretation back to the floor (10 kHz); 512 kbps for the image of the speaker plus 384 kbps for the floor/podium image. (Mouzourakis 2006: 63)

Two new studies took place in 2001 and 2005 at the European Parliament to test a connection through optic fibre (ibid. 64). The results of the first experiment showed that the interpreters were satisfied with the audio and video quality. However, they criticised the selection of pictures and the fact that they did not have a comprehensive view of the conference room (European Parliament Interpretation Directorate 2001: 19–21). Moreover, they stated that they felt uncomfortable and that the remote interpretation setting was overall more tiring (ibid. 22–23). The second experiment, which lasted five weeks, brought similar results: the interpreters were pleased with the audio and video quality although a complete view of the audience was missing. Moreover, they felt alienated and isolated from the conference. The screens caused eye-burning, headaches, lower concentration and higher tension and fatigue. They also stated that they felt their performance to be of inferior quality while working remotely. Medical examinations, however, found no evidence of increased stress, and a performance evaluation confirmed that the interpreters' remote performance was slightly inferior, but not enough to reach statistical relevance (Roziner & Shlesinger 2010: 225–243).

4 Current solutions

4.1 LAN-based solutions

An example of a remote interpreting solution, which is based on a local network is currently being used by the Directorate General for Interpretation of the European Commission (DG SCIC). In this setting, interpreters work from a conventional permanent booth located in another room at the same location, although mobile booths are also used occasionally, in front of which 4 high-resolution screens are placed. Interpreters received the following images via the screens:

- on a 50-inch full HD screen with split view, an overview of the entire meeting table from two different angles is shown; thanks to the big screen and the high resolution, the interpreters are able to see all the participants' faces

- an image of the active speaker is transmitted on two 22-inch full HD screens which are placed laterally to the 50-inch screen

- a static shot of the presidency is displayed on a third 22-inch full-HD screen which is placed on top of the 50-inch screen

In order to transmit the images from the meeting room to the interpreting room, optic fibre cables are used (Technical Compliance Team, DG Interpretation, European Commission 2016).

4.2 External-data-transmission-based solutions

With the growing demand for a more flexible and less costly delivery of interpreting services in a globalized world, several attempts were made in the last decade to make use of technologies, thus overcoming the restrictions of the traditional presence-based scenario with a direct wired connection of all components of the conference system (see §3). For the purpose of this article and from a merely technological point of view, these technologies can be divided into solutions including the transmission of either audio signals only, or the transmission of both audio and video signals to the interpreters.

4.2.1 Audio conferencing solutions

One approach to overcoming existing limitations of bandwidth and thus the impossibility for transmitting sound and image to the interpreters with the required quality (see §3) consists of reducing the transmitted content exclusively to audible signals. The most accessible and therefore most frequently used technology for this transmission relies on the use of telephony. In technical terms, a first rough distinction has to be made between traditional landlines and mobile telephony, as the audible frequencies are mainly being transmitted either via wired connection (landline) or as waves through the air. The use of copper cable and the non-existence of fibre optic connections in certain areas, but also the necessity of handling billions of those connections at a time, still lead to a considerable decrease of the audio frequencies being transmitted to a maximum of 8 kHz, even if landlines today are more often based on digital VoIP technology.[1] Whereas for consecutive interpreting the range of up to 8.000 Hz might be enough (often named 'wideband audio') because of the clear separation of the reception (hearing) and production (talking) processes on the interpreter's side, simultaneous interpreting with listening and talking at the same time is considerably affected by the loss of frequencies due to the masking effect generated by the interpreter's own voice, making incoming frequencies on the same level not audible anymore (Jumpelt 1984). As a result, the physical and cognitive effort of listening will increase. Depending on the frequency of the incoming voice of the speaker and the interpreter's own voice (note that e.g. female and male voices are located in different frequency ranges), the interpreter's output quality will necessarily decrease despite all efforts to compensate for the missing input by interpreting strategies like variation of the voice-to-ear-span or additional pausing. It should not be forgotten that the interpreter has no possibility to compensate for the absence of audible input by visual input when using audio-only solutions. Even if these technologies have improved a lot and specially designed audio bridges allow controlling incoming and outgoing signals with a high level of quality of service even in multilingual scenarios, the above described acoustic parameters cannot be neglected.

4.2.2 Video conferencing solutions

As far as solutions for transmitting sound and image at the same time are concerned, one of the most frequently used technologies is based on video conferencing solutions. These solutions rely on the principle of separately capturing image and sound at the source with camera and microphone, encoding the data with a certain algorithm, transmitting the data packages using one or more parallel lines and decoding the packages again at the destination, making sound and image audible and visible again. These solutions necessarily depend on the availability of adequate and compatible equipment at all source and end points of the communication and the use of a common standard for encoding and decoding of signals (codec). One of the critical points with these video conferencing solutions in terms of quality of simultaneous interpreting is the fact that standard codecs use a compressed file format for transmission of audio signals and compression is carried out either by cutting out certain frequencies, or by other procedures causing similar effects as described before for the audio only solutions.[2]

---

[1] For a comparison of VoIP coding algorithms, see Singh & Mian (2016).
[2] For more information on techniques for video compression, see Wiegand et al. (2003).

5 Technical requirements for remote interpreting

As described above, remote interpreting is a specific method of (conference) interpreting and covers a variety of scenarios of a speaker at a different location from that of the interpreter, enabled by information and communication technology. The main aspect in these scenarios is that the interpreter is not physically present in the same room as all the other actors of the communicative event, thus not having a direct view of either the conference room the conference room, the speaker and/or the audience. To enable interpreters to perform adequately and deliver a quality service, some technical requirements need to be fulfilled. As we have seen before, different experiments have been carried out in order to identify the minimum technical requirements to assure adequate performance quality.

One of the first attempts to define minimal requirements for remote interpreting was the *Code for the use of new technologies in conference interpreting*, which was published by the International Association of Conference Interpreters (AIIC) in 2000 together with other national interpreters' associations, the European Parliament, the European Court of Justice and the joint conference and interpreting service of the European Union and the World Customs Organisation (Korak 2010: 31). AIIC states that interpreters' work conditions in remote settings must comply with the requirements set out in ISO standards 2603 and 4043 (1998 editions, withdrawn in 2016 and replaced with a new set of ISO standards 2603, 4043, 20108 and 20109) which define the work environment of interpreters in mobile and permanent booths. Moreover, the following requirements are to be fulfilled:

- all frequencies between 125 Hz and 12500 Hz are to be transmitted

- interpreters must receive high definition images of the speaker and other participants

- the interpreter shall work no more than two hours per day (AIIC 2000: 2)

A more comprehensive study commissioned by the European Commission was conducted in 2010 by the *Fraunhofer Institut* to evaluate the minimal requirements of video and audio quality for simultaneous interpretation. During this study, conference interpreters were asked to evaluate different audio and video signals to assess the impact of transmission quality on their performance. This study resulted in a guideline:

- all frequencies between 125 Hz and 12500 Hz must be transmitted, although frequencies starting at 75 Hz should also be included in the range

- video quality should be at least 1280×720 at 50 Hz with a ratio of 16:9

- audio must be synchronized (lip synchronization) with the video track with a maximum value of −25 ms or +95 ms

The work of the *Fraunhofer Institut* was used as a starting point to draft the new ISO-Standards 20109 "*Simultaneous interpreting – Equipment – Requirements*" and 20108 "*Simultaneous interpreting – Quality and transmission of sound and image input – Requirements*", which not only raised the minimum requirements, but also added new ones concerning sound and image transmission:

- all frequencies between 125 and 15000 Hz +/−3 dB must be transmitted (ISO 20109:2016: 3)

- image quality must be good enough to avoid blurring and freezing of the video[3]

- audio must be synchronised with the images with a maximum delay of 45 ms or advance of 125 ms

- latency (from the source to the interpreters) must be lower than 500 ms (ISO 20108:2016: 7–8)

6 Future workspace

Based on the technical parameters described in §5, the authors started an experimental research project with the objective of modelling a future workspace for conference interpreters while performing remotely in simultaneous mode. The framework that was chosen for the experimental study was based on a standard working environment for conference interpreters, including, amongst others, a soundproof simultaneous interpreting booth and a hardware interpreter's console as an audio/video interface. The experimental setting was also characterized by some specific markers in terms of interactivity and communication patterns, generally assigned to conference interpreting in literature, such as a mostly monological discourse pattern, interpreting into one language, no possibility for

---

[3] The draft of the ISO-standard 20108 contained more detailed specifications regarding video and transmission requirements: video quality must be at least 720p at 50 Hz or 1080p at 25 Hz, and the signal must be compressed using at least H.264 at 1152 kbps. Moreover, the packet loss value should not exceed 0.2%, jitter should be lower than 15 ms and the latency (roundtrip) in the system shall not exceed 200 ms.

interaction with the speaker during his/her intervention, a symmetric communicative setting with speakers on the same educational level, the same linguistic code used by both speakers, and no variation of speaker's registers (Angelelli 2000: 582–583). All tested scenarios in the experiment were designed for possible implementation in conference interpreting hubs with a basic technical setup similar to the one that can usually be found at conference venues.

6.1 The experiment

The experiment took place in Düsseldorf in collaboration with PCs Professional Conference System GmbH. This experiment aimed to test three different remote interpreting settings:

- using a 65-inch screen with a picture-in-picture function
- using a camera remotely controlled by the interpreter
- using a 360-degree camera and virtual reality glasses

Common to all three parts of the experiment was the text which the interpreters had to interpret in simultaneous mode. Two speakers were asked to talk for a total length of about 10 minutes per scenario. The dialogue was not prepared, but rather improvised and the only rule the speakers had was that the first five minutes of the speech had to be informal and the last five of a more technical nature. According to the Effort Model of Gile (2009) interpreters need to distribute their concentration among the different tasks of simultaneous interpreting, the different degree of difficulty of the speeches aimed to test whether interpreters were still able to operate the new device in the booth under different degrees of stress. The interpreters were not informed about the nature of the text they would have to interpret; this was done to eliminate preparation as a variable from the equation and to assure that they would concentrate on the interpreting effort as well. Moreover, since the interpreters had direct control of the video signals being transmitted, two speakers were intentionally selected in order to force the interpreters to adjust the video settings based on which speaker was talking in order to assure that the new device was actively used during the experiment. The dialogue was held in German and each of the two interpreters was working from their A into their B language. Since the length of each dialogue was only ten minutes and pauses between the scenarios were planned, each interpreter worked alone in the booth while the other was waiting in a separate room to guarantee equal conditions. Moreover, having each interpreter working alone assured that they were forced to operate the additional technological feature while interpreting to determine whether and to what extent this would have an impact on their performance. After the experiment, the interpreters were asked to fill out a questionnaire to evaluate the different settings and technological setups. The questionnaire consisted of 28 questions divided into two parts: first, a more generic part to create a profile of the subjects with questions about their age, experience, language combination and whether or not they already had experience with remote interpreting, and then a second more specific one, in which for each scenario the interpreters were asked to summarize their personal opinion about these new solutions. For example, they were asked whether they could operate the extra devices in the booth, whether they felt they had to put extra effort into it and whether these new solutions were better or poorer than a standard video and audio transmission which they could not control. Moreover, for each scenario they were asked to evaluate the quality of the video transmission on a scale from 1 (poorest) to 5 (best), to share any personal opinion, comment, or criticism and finally to state whether or not they would like to see this solution implemented in the future.

Both the subjects in this study were professional conference interpreters holding a degree in conference interpreting. Both started their career more than 16 years ago and stated having worked as conference interpreters between 51 and 100 days per year, and can therefore be qualified as 'experienced' professional interpreters. In terms of the internal validity of the study, it is also important to mention that they stated having had very little or no experience at all with remote interpreting in conference settings. Due to the very small sample of this study, the results of this experiment cannot be generalized. The primary aim of this pilot study was to test the feasibility of these new technologies. To achieve external validity, the study would have to be reproduced on a larger scale and conducted with an appropriate methodological approach.

6.1.1 Picture-in-picture

The picture-in-picture solution was the first scenario being tested. For this part of the experiment, the speakers were in the conference room, in which two different cameras, each pointed at one speaker, were recording the event. The audio signal was recorded with a wireless microphone and fed together with the video signal to the Extron SMP 351 recording and streaming processor, which streamed the audio and video tracks over the local network of PCs to the interpreting booth. To guarantee lip synchronisation, the audio signal was delayed by 275 ms before being fed to the Extron. In another room, a 65-inch monitor was placed 95 cm from the booth, guaranteeing a distance of roughly 155 cm between the screen and the eyes of the interpreters. According to Causo's guidelines (2011: 2), the booth was placed in such manner that the window' frames of the booth would not obstruct the view of the interpreters. The video signal from the conference room was shown to the interpreters using a picture-in-picture function, meaning that both signals were transmitted simultaneously and that one image occupied a larger portion of the screen while the second video feed was displayed in a smaller format in the bottom right corner and the interpreters were able to switch between the two. According to the draft of the ISO standard 20108[4] (2016: 6), the video signal was reproduced with a resolution of 1920×1080 pixels at 30 frames per seconds (fps).

The results showed that both participants reacted positively to this solution, and they found it to be better than a static video signal, upon which they have no influence. None of the interpreters noticed any increase in workload due to the more technical nature of the second half of the text and stated that they had no problem in using the new device in the booth to switch between the two pictures. Both interpreters stated that they would like to see this solution implemented in the future.

6.1.2 Remote-controlled camera

During the second part of the experiment, the speakers were recorded by only one camera placed in the middle of the conference table. The interpreters were able to remotely move the camera 270 degrees horizontally and 90 degrees vertically on its axes from within the booth. The camera was directly connected to the internal local network of PCs and the interpreters were able to move it using a mouse connected to a laptop in the booth. The audio signal was captured separately using a wireless microphone and delayed by 275 ms before being transferred to the interpreter's booth using a cable. With a resolution of 1080p by 25 fps, this camera respected the indications of the draft of the ISO standard 20108 as well.

The results of the questionnaires showed that this solution was also welcomed by the interpreters. They quickly got used to the control of the camera via mouse and stated that this could rapidly become an automatism. Furthermore, this solution was considered to be better than a non-controllable video transmission. None of the interpreters noticed the difference between the first and second part of the dialogue and had no problem with the camera control.

---

[4]When the experiment was conducted, the final version of the ISO-Norm 20108 had not been published yet. The draft was therefore used for reference.

6.1.3 Virtual reality VR glasses

For the last part of the experiment, the interpreters still worked in a normal interpreting booth wearing Elegiant vr-glasses which use a smartphone (in this case an Apple iPhone SE) to reproduce images. The smartphone was directly connected through Wi-Fi to the 360-degree camera used to capture the dialogue between the two speakers. The audio was captured with a wireless microphone and fed to the interpreting booth using a cable after being delayed by 500 ms. In order to fully exploit the potential of the camera and the vr glasses, the speakers stood in front of each other in a big hall and were asked to move around while talking as well as making use of gestures and mimics.

The interpreters had very different opinions on this solution. The first interpreter found the vr glasses an interesting alternative to a monitor although not very comfortable to wear for a longer period. The subject also stated that, after a short time, one gets used to blindly operating the console in the booth. The second interpreter, on the other hand, was not happy with this solution, finding it tiring for the eyes – it must be noted that the second interpreter wore glasses and because of the design of the vr glasses it was not possible to wear both correction and vr glasses and complained that it was very difficult if not impossible to operate the console in the booth or use a personal computer for terminology research.

At this point, the authors need to clarify that especially this last part of the test was of extremly experimental nature and that the results are not particularly conclusive, also due to the small number of participants. The main goal of this experiment, however, was not to test whether the selected model of vr glasses is ready for a practical application in interpreting boots, but rather to make a first test on operability of vr glasses combined with traditional equipment for simultaneous interpreting in soundproof booths. The results of this test shall be used for additional and more elaborate studies in the future.

6.2 From virtual reality to augmented reality solutions

The experimental study described in §6.1 suggests that the lack of a direct view of the speaker during an event might be compensated for, at least to a certain extent, by the use of technologies that allow the interpreter to control the video input if they feel the need to process non-verbal elements of the content produced by the speakers. Nevertheless, a one-dimensional screen reproducing one or several images will always reduce the possibilities of perception of the setting captured with cameras, as there is still a very clear separation of the interpreter in their remote environment and the room where the original event is taking place. The feeling of separation from the action, often referred to as the feeling of not "being there", might still be big enough to prevent the interpreter from overcoming this psychologically relevant issue.

The last step in the experiment described above was to dive into a virtual reality scenario, making the interpreter feel immersed in the situation, e.g. making similar movements with their eyes and/or their head and body as they would be doing if seated in the room with the speaker and the audience, looking for the necessary visual information to complete the audible content and to render the entire intended message to the listeners. The use of a screen with a double video feed, controlled by the interpreter and reproduced as a picture-in-picture image on a wide screen was accepted by both subjects in the experiment and the additional control task didn't seem to have any negative effect in terms of cognitive overload. However, the use of virtual reality glasses clearly showed that the physical separation from the real world and the traditional equipment placed in it (console for controlling audio input and output, and laptop for document and knowledge management) raises several cognitive and ergonomic issues, although the much more dynamic and self-controlled setting was considered positive as such.

Following this line, the combination of both real and virtual elements in an augmented or mixed reality scenario, where computer-generated images are superimposed on the user's view of the real world, would be the next logical step towards a practical solution for the challenges that remote simultaneous interpreting imposes. AR glasses such as Microsoft's HoloLens, for example, allow projecting images and possibly other virtual images into the vision field of the interpreter, while they can still see and control the real hardware components they need for the delivery of the interpreting service. Any software application used for document and knowledge management could be moved from the real world into the virtual world, projecting only the image of the respective interface into the field of vision and allowing the interpreter to virtually manipulate the application with their hands. Hence, ergonomic aspects such as weight and wearing comfort of the device, cognitive aspects such as real or perceived additional workload and, of course, compliance with the technical parameters set out for distance interpreting, as well as the processing capacity of the processing unit will have to be studied in terms of usability and feasibility.

6.3 Interpreting hub solution

Workspace for conference interpreters working remotely in simultaneous mode should take into account the relevant parameters as stated in existing ISO standards 2603/4043, as far as sound insulation, ventilation and ergonomics are concerned, ISO 20109, as far as equipment for simultaneous interpreting is concerned, and ISO 20108, as far as quality and transmission of sound and image input to interpreters is concerned. Therefore, workspace solutions for distance interpreting should be designed accordingly, assuring that the most important parameters that allow for quality simultaneous interpreting are met.

Even if for economic reasons a solution with the interpreter working from their home office might seem the most obvious and easiest solution, there are several issues that need to be considered when envisaging such solutions. First of all, a dedicated internet connection with assured availability of the necessary bandwidth for transmitting high definition images together with ISO-compliant sound to the interpreter is either not available or hardly affordable for individuals. In addition, home office rooms would have to be equipped either with an appropriate interpreting booth or with components assuring compliance with the main parameters of ISO 2603/4043 in terms of e.g. insulation and ventilation. A lack of possibilities for dynamic control of the Internet connection while interpreting, as well as data protection and confidentiality issues would also have to be resolved if home office workspace were to be used.

Particularly for multilingual events with more than two languages being spoken and interpreted at the same time, a promising approach in terms of Quality of Service both from technical and interpreting performance views are solutions with interpreting being performed in specially designed hubs, where interpreters would find all the necessary working conditions to deliver quality interpreting. Traditional ISO compliant booths as a minimum standard, or a specifically designed workspace ensuring the basic requirements. This should be equipped with state-of-the-art digital interpreting equipment, dedicated internet connections with permanently available bandwidth, controlled ambient conditions with active regulation of air supply and carbon dioxide levels as well as immersive 3D environments with high resolution projection screens. Interpreters should be able to choose the desired visual input out of several video feeds, AR components; technical support available on site would set the appropriate technical framework. In addition, offices with access to online and offline information sources for preparation before and during the event, rest rooms for relaxation and lounge areas for the necessary professional and social exchange within the interpreting team, would help to overcome the alienation perceived by interpreters working in remote scenarios and environments that have not been developed specifically for this purpose.

Apart from these more technical aspects, any kind of hub solution would also have to address psychological factors such as measurable or perceived stress. Moser-Mercer (2005: 15) states that "it appears that (...) interpreters seem to be under increased psychological stress when working away from the conference room, mostly because they experience a lack of control of the situation". Even if there are no studies available yet that would explain exactly which kind of control interpreters are missing,[5] aspects such as those given below are what interpreters feel they need to control

- availability of a technician in case of technical problems

- the interaction with team mates working in the same interpreting booth or across booths in multilingual conferences

- the (sometimes very limited or even non-existing) possibility of talking to speakers and audience before the conference or during breaks

- self-control of the direction of sight, focusing on speaker audience, presentation or any other visual input available

The design of an interpreting hub as described above could easily cover the first two aspects. A hub would need the presence of a technician onsite in the hub to manage the technical equipment and the whole team (if interpreting takes place from one hub only) or at least the booth mates would be working together at the same place. The interaction and communication with speakers and audience would, of course, require a specific solution, but could be handled, e.g. considering 'institutionalized' briefing and Q&A sessions before, during and after the meeting.

Control of the view on the speaker, audience and additional visual input, such as presentations, in presence-based interpreting usually performed by head movements and eye focusing would need further development based on the technologies described in §6.1. Considering the rapid development of image captioning, transmission and reproduction, it seems only a matter of time until these technologies will be affordable and adaptedn to the needs of remote simultaneous conference interpreting.

---

[5]Note that, apart from the interpreter's console with standard control buttons for the incoming sound, an interpreter in a presence-based conference setting also has only limited control of the actions in the room.

7 Conclusions

In times of growing demand for flexible, accessible and customer-oriented digitalized communication services in a globalized world, technological solutions for quality simultaneous interpreting services will have to be developed, taking into account several aspects related to the organization and delivery of those services. Existing standard solutions developed for other purposes, such as video conferencing or web conferencing without interpreting, or solutions for consecutive interpreting in specializations other than conference interpreting appear not to be sophisticated enough to meet the special requirements that distance interpreting imposes in terms of sound and image input to interpreters in bilingual and multilingual conference settings. Technological enhancements in the field of virtual reality and augmented reality, as well as immersive communication environments, may offer the possibility to overcome existing constraints.

One of the major challenges for interpreting studies in the field of distance interpreting will be finding a more interdisciplinary and future-oriented approach, building teams of researchers in the technical, medical and psychological field, to name only a few of them, and to combine these different research disciplines in multidisciplinary projects that can actively lead to designing the future workspace for conference interpreters in the first place, and for other specialized interpreting services as well. It goes without saying that fellow (conference) interpreters need to be prepared for remote simultaneous interpreting during their training, as this modality is experiencing a growing demand in different interpreting specializations, including tele- and videoconference interpreting (Braun 2015). Apart from the integration of training modules designed specifically for this modality, addressing cognitive, communicative and technical aspects, amongst others, this would also require adequate equipment of training facilities with the appropriate features (audio/video conferencing hard- and software and connectivity, to mention just a few of them).

References

AIIC. 2000. *Code for the use of new technologies in conference interpretation.* http://www.staff.uni-mainz.de/fantinuo/class/files/cai/aiic_code_interpreting%20technologies.pdf, accessed 2017-10-31.

Andres, Dörte & Stefanie Falk. 2009. Information and communication technologies (ICT) in interpreting: Remote and telephone interpreting. In Dörte Andres & Sonja Pöllabauer (eds.), *Spürst Du wie der Bauch rauf-runter? Fachdolmetschen im Gesundheitsbereich* (InterPartes), 9–27. München: Martin Meidenbauer.

Angelelli, Claudia. 2000. Interpretation as a communicative event: A look through hymes' lenses. *Meta* 45(4). 580–592.

AVIDICUS project. 2008–2011. *AVIDICUS 1 (2008–11)*. http://wp.videoconference-interpreting.net/?page_id=13, accessed 2018-5-12.

AVIDICUS project. 2011–2013. *AVIDICUS 2 (2011–13)*. http://wp.videoconference-interpreting.net/?page_id=16, accessed 2018-5-12.

AVIDICUS project. 2014–2016. *AVIDICUS 3 (2014–16)*. http://wp.videoconference-interpreting.net/?page_id=154, accessed 2018-5-12.

Braun, Sabine. 2015. Remote interpreting. In Holly Mikkelson & Renée Jourdenais (eds.), *Routledge handbook of interpreting*. Abingdon/New York: Routledge.

Braun, Sabine & Judith L. Taylor. 2011. Video-mediated interpreting: An overview of current practice and research. In Sabine Braun & Judith L. Taylor (eds.), *Videoconference and remote interpreting in criminal proceedings*, 25–57. Guilford: University of Surrey.

Causo, José Esteban. 2011. Technical guidelines for remote interpretation. In Sabine Braun & Judith L. Taylor (eds.), *Videoconference and remote interpreting in criminal proceedings*, 301–306. Guilford: University of Surrey.

Chernov, Ghelly V. 2004. *Interference and anticipation in simultaneous interpreting: A probability-prediction model.* Amsterdam/Philadelphia: John Benjamin.

European Parliament Interpretation Directorate. 2001. *Report on remote interpretation test, 22-25 January 2001.* Brussels. http://www.europarl.europa.eu/interp/remote_interpreting/ep_report1.pdf, accessed 2017-12-29.

Gile, Daniel. 2009. *Basic concepts and models for interpreter and translator training.* Amsterdam/Philadelphia: John Benjamins.

ISO 20108:2016. 2016. *Simultaneous interpreting – quality and transmission of sound and image input – requirements.* Standard. International Organization for Standardization.

ISO 20109:2016. 2016. *Simultaneous interpreting – equipment – requirements.* Standard. International Organization for Standardization.

ISO 2603:2016. 2016. *Simultaneous interpreting – permanent booths – requirements.* Standard. International Organization for Standardization.

ISO 4043:2016. 2016. *Simultaneous interpreting – mobile booths – requirements.* Standard. International Organization for Standardization.

Jumpelt, Walter. 1984. Die Arbeitswelt des Konferenzdolmetschers nach neuen ISO- und IEC-Normen. *Lebende Sprachen* 29(1). 1–5.

Korak, Christina. 2010. *Remote interpreting via Skype: Anwendungsmöglichkeiten von VoIP-Software im Bereich Community Interpreting: Communicate everywhere?* Berlin: Frank & Timme.

Kurz, Ingrid. 2000. Tagungsort Genf/Nairobi/Wien: Zu einigen Aspekten des Teledolmetschens. In Midra Kadric, Klaus Kaindl & Franz Pöchhacker (eds.), *Translationswissenschaft: Festschrift für Mary Snell-Hornby zum 60. Geburtstag*, 291–302. Tübingen: Stauffenburg Festschriften.

Luisetto, Martina. 2016. Visueller Input beim Remote Interpreting: Eine empirische Untersuchung zum Einfluss des visuellen Inputs auf die Qualität des Dolmetschprodukts beim Remote Interpreting anhand des Sprachenpaars Deutsch-Italienisch. In Ursula Gross-Dinter (ed.), *Dolmetschen 3.0 – Einblicke in einen Beruf im Wandel*, 51–92. Berlin: Frank & Timme.

Moser-Mercer, Barbara. 2003. *Remote interpreting: Assessment of human factors and performance parameters.* https://aiic.net/page/1125/remote-interpreting-assessment-of-human-factors-and-pe/lang/1, accessed 2017-10-31.

Moser-Mercer, Barbara. 2005. Remote interpreting: Issues of multi-sensory integration in a multilingual task. *Meta* 50(2). 727–738.

Mouzourakis, Panayotis. 1996. Videoconferencing: Techniques and challenges. *Interpreting* 1(1). 21–38.

Mouzourakis, Panayotis. 2006. Remote interpreting: A technical perspective on recent experiments. *Interpreting* 8(1). 45–66.

Rennert, Sylvi. 2008. Visual input in simultaneous interpreting. *Meta* 53(1). 204–217.

Roziner, Ilan & Miriam Shlesinger. 2010. Much ado about something remote: Stress and performance in remote interpreting. *Interpreting* 12(2). 214–247.

Singh, Hardeep & M Mian. 2016. Comparative study and analysis of various VoIP coding algorithms. *International Journal of Computer Applications* 141. 6–10.

Technical Compliance Team, DG Interpretation, European Commission. 2016. *Internal archives of the European Union.*

TechTarget Network. 2017. http://searchunifiedcommunications.techtarget.com/definitions/page/7, accessed 2017-10-31.

UNESCO. 1987. *Management of interpretation services in the United Nations system. Report of the United Nations joint inspection unit.* http://unesdoc.unesco.org/images/0007/000732/073286eo.pdf, accessed 2018-5-12.

Wiegand, Thomas, Gary J. Sullivan, Gisle Bjøntegaard & Ajay Luthra. 2003. Overview of the h.264/AVC video coding standard. In IEEE Transactions (ed.), *Circuits and systems for video technology*, 560–576.

Name index

Abril Martí, Isabel, 108, 110
Alessandrini, Maria Serena, 15
Andres, Dörte, 5, 124
Angelelli, Claudia, 95, 110, 130

Baigorri Jalón, Jesús, 2
Balogh, Katalin, 93
Barik, Henri C., 52
Bartłomiejczyk, Magdalena, 52, 65
Berber, Diana-Cristina, 65
Berk-Seligson, Susan, 95
Besnier, Jean-Michel, 7
Biagini, Giulio, 31
Bonner, William, 98
Bot, Hanneke, 95
Braun, Sabine, 15, 19, 21, 91–93, 109–111, 121, 124, 137

Carabelli, Angela, 64
Causo, José Esteban, 5, 131
Chang, Chia-chien, 2
Chernov, Ghelly V., 120, 124
Clarici, Andrea, 15, 19, 21
Collard, Camille, 15
Corpas Pastor, Gloria, 14
Costa, Hernani, 17, 30

de Manuel Jerez, Jesús, 63–66
De Merulis, Gianpiero, 31
Defrancq, Bart, 15
Deng, Li, 17
Devaux, Jérôme, 94, 98, 99, 102, 111

Ellis, Ronald, 94

Falk, Stefanie, 5, 124
Fantinuoli, Claudio, 2, 4, 14, 17, 18, 30, 31, 40
Feinauer, A. E., 67
Fern, Lily May, 14
Finn, Ed, 3
Fowler, Yvonne, 63, 64, 94, 109, 111
Fullwood, Chris, 93

Galimberti, Umberto, 3
Gentile, Adolfo, 95
Gentile, Paola, 2
Gile, Daniel, 2, 14, 16, 20, 26, 32, 52, 65, 130
Goldsmith, Josh, 14
Gorm Hansen, Inge, 62
Grbic, Nadja, 95

Haas, Aaron, 93
Hale, Sandra, 95
Hertog, Eric, 93
Hodges, Louise, 93, 108
Huws, Ursula, 7

Johnson, Molly, 92
Jones, Roderick, 16
Jumpelt, Walter, 127

Kahneman, Daniel, 32
Kantowitz, Barry H., 32
Knight, J. L., 32

Name index

Korak, Christina, 128
Korpal, Pawel, 15
Kurz, Ingrid, 120, 123

Lamberger-Felber, Heike, 16, 22
Laster, Kathy, 95
Latour, Bruno, 98
Lee, Jieun, 110
Lee, Robert, 92, 95–97, 110
Lee, Yun-Hyang, 62, 64
Lesch, Harold, 70
Licoppe, Christian, 93
Lim, Lily, 62, 65
Llewellyn-Jones, Peter, 92, 95–97, 110
Luisetto, Martina, 123

Martin, Anne, 95, 108, 110
Mason, Ian, 95
Mazza, Cristina, 15, 16, 19, 23, 25
McKay, Carolyn, 93
Mead, Peter, 15, 16
Merlini, Raffaela, 108
Mian, M, 127
Mikkelson, Holly, 95
Miler-Cassino, Joanna, 93
Moorad, I., 69
Moser-Mercer, Barbara, 122–124, 136
Motta, Manuela, 67
Mouzourakis, Panayotis, 120, 123–125
Müller, Markus, 6

Napier, Jemina, 109
Nartowska, Karolina, 95
Neufeind, Max, 7
Niska, Helge, 94

Orlando, Mark, 14
Ortega Herráez, Juan Miguel, 95

Pernice, Kara, 3

Pinazo, E. Postigo, 62–65
Pinochi, Diletta, 15, 16, 21, 23, 25
Plotnikoff, Joyce, 91, 93
Pöchhacker, Franz, 64
Prandi, Bianca, 31, 40, 42
Pym, Anthony, 8

Radburn-Remfry, Patricia, 92, 93, 108
Regehr, Glenn, 63
Rennert, Sylvi, 123
Riccardi, Alessandra, 63, 64
Rombouts, Dirk, 93, 109
Rosenberg, Brett Allen, 110
Ross, Bella, 3
Roth, Michael, 93
Roziner, Ilan, 120, 123, 125
Rütten, Anja, 30
Rybińska, Zofia, 93

Sandrelli, Annalisa, 62–67
Seeber, Kilian G., 14–16, 34, 35, 43
Seidman, Irving, 98
Seleskovitch, Danica, 16
Setton, Robin, 16
Shlesinger, Miriam, 62, 120, 123, 125
Singh, Hardeep, 127
Stewart, Craig, 4

Takeda, Kayoko, 2
Taylor, Judith L., 124
Taylor, Veronica, 95
Thaxton, Ronnie, 92, 93
Timarová, Šárka, 15

van den Hoogen, Ronald, 108
van Rotterdam, Peter, 108
Verdier, Maud, 93

Wadensjö, Cecilia, 49, 95
Wickens, Christopher D., 32, 33

Wiegand, Thomas, 127
Wiggins, Elizabeth, 92
Will, Martin, 17, 30
Woolfson, Richard, 91, 93

Xu, Ran, 2, 31

Yu, Dong, 17

Zanettin, Federico, 3

Language index

Afrikaans, 68^4, 71, 74
Arabic, 98

Chinese, 98

English, 15, 16, 21, 41–43, 44^{10}, 68^4, 71^7, 71, 75, 94

French, 19, 20, 22, 124

German, 15, 16, 19, 20, 22, 41, 42, 47, 130

isiNdebele, 68^4, 71, 74, 75
isiXhosa, 68^4
isiZulu, 68^4, 71, 74, 75
Italian, 15, 41, 42

Sepedi, 68^4, 71, 74
Sesotho, 68^4, 71, 74
Setswana, 68^4, 75
SiSwati, 68^4, 71, 74

Tshivenda, 68^4, 71, 74
Turkish, 98

Xitsonga, 68^4

Subject index

360-degree camera, 130, 133

advanced search, 30
audibility, 81
augmented reality, 10, 120, 137
automatic speech translation, 5, 6
Avidicus, 92^1, 92–94, 109, 111

bigram, 49^{11}, 49
Black Box, 9, 62^1, 62, 64, 65^3, 65–70, 73–76, 82
body language, 93, 94, 96, 100, 101, 108

chuchotage, 2
co-located party, 104, 110
cognitive load, 9, 16, 17, 24, 25, 37, 44, 48, 56, 57, 122
Cognitive Load Model, 36
cognitive overload, 37, 41, 134
Cognitive Resource Footprint, 33, 37, 40
communicative event, 121, 122, 128
computer-assisted interpreting, 4, 17, 29, 56
conference room, 14, 18, 25, 125, 128, 131, 132, 136
control setting, 22, 25
court, 1, 10, 72, 84, 92, 93, 95, 97, 98, 100–102, 104, 105, 108–112
court actor, 94
court hearing, 92, 93, 95, 96, 98, 102, 108

court interpreter, 94–96, 98, 104, 112
courtroom, 92, 109, 111
cultural acceptability, 108, 109

defendant, 92^2, 92, 93, 97, 99–102, 104, 105, 108–110
delivery rate, 15, 20
demand vector, 34, 40

electronic glossary, 36, 37
equipment, 2, 4, 10, 17, 65^3, 91–94, 98, 100, 101, 104, 105, 108–111, 127, 133–137
error reduction, 22, 25
expert assessor post-experiment, 68

freelance, 62, 64, 72

glossary, 37, 40–44, 46–50, 53, 56, 57
glossary query, 47–50, 53, 56
glossary search, 56
group post-experiment, 68

high definition, 120, 128, 135
human interpreter, 4, 14

idiomatic, 79, 83
idiomatic language, 83
in-house training, 68, 72, 84
information density, 16, 20
inter-subject variability, 46, 52
interaction management, 10, 94, 96, 101, 102, 104, 105, 110, 111

Subject index

interference score, 35, 40
interpretation quality, 20, 64
InterpretBank, 30, 40, 42, 43, 49, 50, 53, 56
interpreter, 4, 8, 9, 14–18, 22, 25, 29, 30, 32, 36, 37, 48, 50, 62–67, 70, 72, 83, 84, 92^2, 92, 94–96, 98–102, 109–112, 120–122, 127–130, 132–135, 136^5
interpreter training, 8, 61, 62^1, 62–65, 84, 92
interpreting booth, 129, 131, 133, 135, 136
interpreting curriculum, 62
interpreting equipment, 135
interpreting exercise, 74
interpreting hub, 136
interpreting modality, 119
interpreting performance, 4, 10, 68, 71, 75, 76, 79–81, 85, 87, 88, 100, 135
interpreting practice, 2, 67
interpreting process, 4, 17, 30, 37, 41, 96
interpreting quality, 17, 93
interpreting service, 128, 134
interpreting session, 82, 83, 85
intonation, 81, 83

lip synchronization, 120, 129
listening, 101
local cognitive load, 41

machine translation, 5, 6, 7^7, 13
macro error, 79–81
matching method, 70, 71, 73
micro error, 81
microphone, 86, 99, 111, 127, 131–133
minimal latency, 18, 25

mock-up system, 9, 18, 22, 25
monolingual, 92, 94
monolingual setting, 92, 93
morphological complexity, 43, 49, 50, 56
multilingual, 30, 92–94, 127, 135–137

open-ended question, 72, 80
output quality, 9, 127

paraphrase, 53
Parliament, 9, 15, 62, 67^4, 67–69, 70^5, 70, 71^7, 72, 74, 75, 84, 125, 128
participant alignment, 10, 95, 96, 109, 111
pause, 83, 85
perceptual-cognitive stage, 34
picture-in-picture function, 130, 132
precise rendition, 48, 50
presence-based scenario, 121, 126
professional interpreter, 62, 64, 67, 70
proven interpretation, 119

remote defendant, 92, 93, 104
remote interpretation, 119, 125
remote interpreting, 9
remote party, 100, 104, 109, 110
rendition, 15, 26, 32, 34, 48, 50, 52
respondent, 72, 74, 77, 79–81
role-space model, 95, 96, 98, 102^6, 102, 105

second interpreter, 133
self-assessment, 78
self-assessment grid, 74
self-assessment session, 75, 76, 80, 82
simultaneous conference interpreting, 123, 136
simultaneous interpretation, 2, 4, 5, 18, 31, 128

simultaneous interpreting, 56
simultaneous mode, 10, 129, 130, 135
Skype, 6, 98[5], 98, 111
soundproof, 129, 133
source language, 20–23, 43, 53
source text, 14, 15, 66, 122
speech recognition, 4–6, 9, 31, 40, 57
split role, 10
split role-space, 105
spreadsheet, 40, 43
stimulus, 21, 25, 34, 36, 43, 44, 48, 70, 74, 75
student interpreter, 64, 65
synchronisation, 93, 131

target language, 5, 6, 15, 16, 21, 34, 37, 43, 80, 81, 83, 85, 86, 122
technological support, 13–15, 18, 20–22, 24, 25
technological turn, 3, 4, 6, 11
telephony, 126
terminological challenge, 121
terminological challenges, 10
terminological database, 36
terminological information, 4
terminological precision, 30, 50
terminological quality, 30, 31, 41, 46, 56
terminological query, 37
terminological search, 32
terminological support, 17
terminological unit, 52
terminology, 4, 14, 17, 19, 29, 41, 43, 52, 56, 72, 81, 85, 86, 101, 121, 133
terminology management, 17, 30, 31, 36, 40, 42, 46, 56
terminology search, 9
trigram, 44, 49[11], 49

true-to-life experience, 108

unigram, 49

video quality, 93, 94, 124, 125, 129[3], 129
video signal, 124, 131, 132
videoconference, 4, 91, 121, 137
videoconference communication, 121, 122
virtual reality, 120, 130, 134, 137
visual input, 16, 26, 122, 123, 127, 135, 136

world knowledge, 53